DURHAM
Travel Guide
2025

A Definitive local guide to Top
Attractions, Hidden Gems,
Culinary Delights & Essential Tips
for Every Traveler in Durham
England

Robert I. Manley

COPYRIGHT

Table of Content

Forward

I still remember the first time I stepped foot in Durham. It was a crisp autumn morning, and the scent of damp cobblestone mixed with the faint aroma of fresh-brewed coffee from a tucked-away café. As I wandered through the winding streets, the towering silhouette of **Durham Cathedral** came into view, bathed in golden light. It was at that moment I knew—Durham was special.

Over the years, my connection with this city has only deepened. Whether it was losing track of time in the **Palace Green Library**, discovering a hidden alehouse with locals who welcomed me like an old friend, or standing in awe beneath the centuries-old **arches of Durham Castle**, every visit brought new surprises. Durham isn't just a place you pass through—it's a place that leaves its mark on you.

This book was born out of my passion for sharing those experiences. I wanted to create more than just a travel guide; I wanted to give you a **personal invitation** to uncover Durham's magic in a way that feels like you're exploring it with a friend. Each page is crafted with **insider tips, personal discoveries,** and hidden corners that most tourists overlook.

If you love history, you'll lose yourself in tales of Norman kings, medieval monks, and miners who shaped the city's heart. If you're an adventurer, the Durham Dales, coastal walks, and kayak-friendly River Wear are calling your name. And if you're here for the food? Well, let's just say Durham's hearty pub meals, charming tea rooms, and Michelin-starred dining will not disappoint.

But this book isn't just about ticking off landmarks. It's about immersing yourself in Durham's rhythm, strolling along the riverbanks at sunset, listening to street musicians in the Market Square, or sharing a pint with a stranger who quickly becomes a friend. Durham has a way of welcoming you home, even if it's your first time here.

So whether you're visiting for a weekend or planning an extended stay, I hope this guide helps you fall in love with Durham the way I did. Let's explore together.

Welcome to Durham

The first time I set foot in Durham, I felt as if I had stepped into a living postcard—a place where history whispers from ancient stone walls, and the air carries the soft murmur of the River Wear as it winds around the city like a protective embrace. There's something undeniably magical about this historic gem in Northeast England.

Nestled between rolling green hills and a meandering river, Durham is a city that effortlessly weaves together the old and the new. It's a place where grand medieval architecture stands tall against a backdrop of modern vibrancy, where bustling markets are set in the shadow of a UNESCO-listed cathedral, and where cobbled streets lead to hidden courtyards brimming with stories.

Durham is more than just a picturesque city; it's a place of deep cultural and historical significance, with roots stretching back over a thousand years. From its origins as a religious sanctuary to its legacy as a stronghold of learning and heritage, Durham has evolved into one of England's most captivating destinations. Whether you're here for history, adventure, food, or simply a peaceful escape, Durham has something to offer.

Why Visit Durham in 2025?

As the world rediscovers the joy of travel, there has never been a better time to visit Durham. In 2025, this city promises to be a vibrant blend of tradition and modernity, with new attractions, enhanced cultural experiences, and a fresh wave of energy from locals and visitors alike.

- **A Renaissance in Heritage and Tourism** – Durham's iconic landmarks, from its world-renowned **Durham Cathedral** to the historic **Durham Castle**, continue to be meticulously preserved. In 2025, expect newly curated exhibits, guided tours with augmented reality, and enhanced visitor experiences that make history feel more alive than ever.
- **Exciting Cultural and Seasonal Events** – If you time your visit right, you can witness the **Lumiere Festival**, a dazzling light spectacle that transforms the cityscape, or the traditional **Durham Miners' Gala**, a celebration of working-class heritage.

- **Nature and Outdoor Adventures** – The **Durham Dales** and **Durham Heritage Coast** offer breathtaking landscapes for hiking, cycling, and photography enthusiasts. The city itself is home to stunning riverside walks and hidden green spaces that make for perfect, serene getaways.
- **A Culinary Evolution** – Durham's food scene is evolving rapidly, with innovative eateries serving up local delicacies alongside global flavors. From cozy pubs with roaring fires to Michelin-guide-worthy dining experiences, 2025 will be an exciting year for food lovers.

Whether you're a first-time traveler or a returning visitor, Durham in 2025 offers something fresh, making it a must-visit destination.

A Brief History of Durham

Durham's story is a tapestry woven with faith, power, and resilience. It all began in **995 AD**, when a group of monks carrying the relics of **St. Cuthbert** arrived at this natural peninsula, seeking a resting place safe from Viking invasions. Legend has it that the saint's body miraculously became immovable, signifying that Durham was destined to be his final home. Thus, a grand cathedral was built in his honor, and the city grew around it.

Throughout the medieval period, Durham was a powerful religious and political center. The **Prince-Bishops of Durham**, ruling with almost king-like authority, fortified the city and established it as a major seat of power in Northern England. This influence is still evident today in the towering battlements of **Durham Castle**, which served as a stronghold against Scottish invasions.

Fast forward to the Industrial Revolution, and Durham's coal mining industry became the heart of its economy, shaping the city's working-class identity. The proud mining heritage lives on in annual traditions such as the **Durham Miners' Gala**, one of the most important labor festivals in Europe.

Today, Durham has embraced modernity while fiercely preserving its heritage. As a **university city**, it thrives with youthful energy, intellectual vibrancy, and a dynamic cultural scene. The blend of medieval streets, historic traditions, and a forward-looking spirit makes Durham a city like no other.

Durham's Unique Charm

One of the most remarkable things about Durham is how it balances grandeur with intimacy. It's a city that captivates both from a distance and up close.

- **Architectural Marvels** – Durham Cathedral, a **UNESCO World Heritage Site**, is considered one of the greatest Norman structures in the world. Walking through its massive stone nave, you can't help but feel awed by the intricate craftsmanship. Just across Palace Green, **Durham Castle**, now part of **Durham University**, offers a striking contrast—its imposing medieval fortress exterior houses an interior filled with centuries of stories.

- **The Living Culture of Durham** – Durham isn't just about ancient stones; it's about the people who breathe life into them. The city's market square buzzes with local artisans, street performers, and storytellers who keep the city's traditions alive. From folk music sessions in cozy pubs to contemporary art exhibitions, Durham seamlessly blends old-world charm with modern creativity.

- **Nature's Embrace** – Beyond its historic streets, Durham is surrounded by stunning landscapes. The **River Wear**, which loops around the city like a silver ribbon, offers idyllic walking paths with scenic views of the cathedral rising above the trees. Venture just beyond the city, and you'll find the rolling **Durham Dales**, dotted with charming villages, waterfalls, and endless green pastures.

Durham is a city where every corner has a story, and every street invites you to slow down and soak in its timeless beauty.

How to Use This Guide

This travel guide is designed to be your **companion to Durham**, whether you're here for a weekend getaway, a week-long adventure, or even just planning your visit from afar. Here's how to make the most of it:

1. **Explore Chapter by Chapter** – We've structured this guide to take you from the essentials—how to get here and where to stay—to the deep cultural and historical layers that make Durham special.

2. **Discover Hidden Gems** – Beyond the well-known landmarks, we'll take you to off-the-beaten-path spots, secret courtyards, and lesser-known experiences that only locals talk about.
3. **Plan According to Your Interests** – Whether you're a history buff, nature lover, foodie, or adventure seeker, we've tailored sections to cater to all types of travelers.
4. **Get Practical Tips** – From the best seasons to visit to navigating the city with ease, we'll equip you with **everything you need for a seamless trip**.

Final Thoughts

Durham is a place that **stays with you long after you've left**. It's a city where time slows down, allowing you to savor its rich history, its stunning landscapes, and its warm, welcoming atmosphere.

So whether you're drawn by the **majestic cathedral**, the **legendary tales of the Prince-Bishops**, the **vibrant cultural scene**, or simply the **promise of a peaceful riverside stroll, Durham awaits**—ready to surprise, inspire, and captivate you.

Getting to Durham

Getting to Durham is a straightforward and enjoyable experience, no matter how you choose to travel. Whether you're flying in from another country, taking a scenic train ride through the British countryside, or driving along picturesque roads, the journey itself can be part of the adventure. In this chapter, I'll guide you through the best travel options to Durham in 2025, offering clear and practical advice to make your trip smooth and stress-free.

By Air: Nearest Airports & Best Flight Options

If you're traveling to Durham from outside the UK—or even from a distant part of Britain—your best option might be to **fly into one of the nearby airports**. While Durham doesn't have its own airport, there are several well-connected options just a short drive or train ride away.

Nearest Airports to Durham

1. **Newcastle International Airport (NCL) – Best Choice**

- Distance from Durham: 25 miles (40 km)
- Travel Time to Durham: 30-40 minutes by train or car
- Best for: International and domestic flights from major UK and European cities
- How to Get to Durham from Newcastle Airport:
  - By Train: The quickest option—take the Metro from the airport to Newcastle Central Station, then a direct train to Durham (15-20 minutes).
  - By Car/Taxi: A taxi or rental car takes about 30 minutes via the A1(M) motorway.

2. Teesside International Airport (MME) – Smaller but Convenient
   - Distance from Durham: 22 miles (35 km)
   - Travel Time to Durham: 35-45 minutes by car or taxi
   - Best for: Flights from London, Aberdeen, and select European destinations

- How to Get to Durham from
  Teesside Airport:
  - By Car/Taxi: The fastest
    route is along the A1(M)
    or A167.
  - By Train: Take a taxi to
    Darlington Station,
    then a quick train to
    Durham.
3. Leeds Bradford Airport (LBA) – A
   Wider Range of Flights
   - Distance from Durham: 80
     miles (129 km)
   - Travel Time to Durham:
     Around 1.5 hours by train or car
   - Best for: International travelers
     who can't find a direct flight to
     Newcastle
   - How to Get to Durham from
     Leeds Bradford Airport:
     - By Train: Take a train
       from Leeds Station to
       Durham (1 hour).
     - By Car: Drive via the
       A1(M), a straightforward
       and scenic motorway
       journey.

Flight Tips for 2025 Travelers

- If you're flying from overseas, **Newcastle Airport is the best choice** due to its easy connections to Durham.
- Consider budget airlines like **Ryanair, EasyJet, and Jet2**, which frequently fly into Newcastle and Leeds.
- Book your flight early—**at least 2-3 months in advance**—for the best deals on both domestic and international routes.

By Train: Rail Connections from London, Edinburgh & Other Cities

Durham is **one of the best-connected cities by rail in the UK**, making train travel one of the most convenient and scenic ways to arrive.

Major Train Routes to Durham

1. **From London** (King's Cross Station)
   - **Travel Time:** Around 2 hours 45 minutes
   - **Train Operator:** LNER (London North Eastern Railway)
   - **Tips:** Opt for an **Advance Ticket** for lower fares, and book

a seat on the **right-hand side** for stunning countryside views!

2. **From Edinburgh**
   - **Travel Time:** 1 hour 45 minutes
   - **Train Operators:** LNER, CrossCountry, TransPennine Express
   - **Tips:** If you're visiting Scotland before Durham, this train ride offers breathtaking views of the coastline.

3. **From Manchester**
   - **Travel Time:** 2.5 to 3 hours
   - **Train Operators:** TransPennine Express
   - **Tips:** Book a **direct train** to avoid unnecessary stops or changes.

4. **From Newcastle**
   - **Travel Time:** 15 minutes
   - **Train Operators:** LNER, Northern Rail
   - **Tips:** Trains run **every 10-15 minutes**, making it the easiest way to reach Durham from Newcastle.

Arriving at Durham Station

Durham's **historic railway station** is located on a hill, offering **a breathtaking first glimpse of Durham Cathedral** as you step out. From here, you can:

- **Walk into the city centre** in 10 minutes (downhill).
- **Take a taxi or bus** if you have heavy luggage.

By Car: Driving Routes, Parking, and Scenic Drives

If you enjoy **road trips** or prefer the flexibility of driving, Durham is easily accessible by car.

Best Driving Routes to Durham

- **From London:** 5-hour drive via the **A1(M) motorway** (fastest route).
- **From Edinburgh:** 2.5-hour drive via the **A1 coastal route** (scenic).
- **From Manchester:** 2.5-hour drive via the **M62 and A1(M)**.

Parking in Durham

Durham is a compact city with **limited central parking**, so it's best to use **Park and Ride services** located outside the city.

- **Belmont Park & Ride:** Ideal for visitors arriving from the A1(M).
- **Sniperley Park & Ride:** Great for those coming from the west.
- **City Centre Parking:** Available but expensive—best for short stays.

Scenic Drives Near Durham

- **Durham Dales & Pennines Route** – Explore **High Force Waterfall** and quaint villages.
- **Heritage Coast Drive** – A stunning coastal route towards **Seaham and Sunderland**.

By Bus: National Express, Local Buses & Private Coach Services

For budget-conscious travelers, buses offer a **cost-effective** way to reach Durham.

National Express & Megabus

- **From London:** 6-7 hours (direct or via Newcastle).
- **From Manchester & Leeds:** Around 3-4 hours.
- **From Edinburgh:** 3-4 hours.

Local Buses & Coaches

- **From Newcastle:** Regular buses (Arriva, Go North East) take **30-40 minutes**.
- **From Teesside & Middlesbrough:** Hourly services available.

Best Bus Tip:

If you're coming from a nearby city, trains are **much faster**, but if you're on a tight budget, **Megabus and National Express** offer great deals.

Sustainable Travel Options

For eco-conscious travelers, Durham offers several **sustainable travel options**.

Electric Vehicle Travel

- Charging points available in city car parks.
- Durham aims to be a **low-emission zone** by 2025.

Cycling to Durham

- The **National Cycle Network (NCN1 & NCN14)** passes through Durham, making it **bike-friendly**.

Trains & Buses – The Greenest Choice

- Trains produce **far lower carbon emissions** than cars or flights.
- Durham's **public transport network** is being improved for 2025, including more **electric buses**.

Final Thoughts

Whether you fly, drive, or take a scenic train ride, **Durham is easy to reach and well worth the journey**. With so many travel options, you can choose the one that best suits your budget, comfort, and sustainability goals.

Now that you know how to get here, let's dive into Getting **Around Durham** in the next chapter!

Getting Around Durham

Once you've arrived in Durham, getting around the city is a breeze. This charming, compact city is designed for easy exploration, whether you prefer walking through its historic streets, cycling along scenic river paths, or hopping on a bus for a quick ride. From convenient public transport to accessible facilities, this guide will ensure you make the most of your time in Durham.

Public Transport: Bus Routes, Taxi Services & Ride-Sharing

Buses: The Most Affordable Way to Travel

Durham's public bus system is reliable, affordable, and easy to use. If you're staying a bit outside the city centre or want to visit nearby villages, the bus is your best option.

Key Bus Operators in Durham

1. **Go North East** – Covers most routes in and around Durham, including connections to Newcastle, Sunderland, and Gateshead.

2. **Arriva North East** – Serves routes to Teesside, Bishop Auckland, and Darlington.
3. **Durham Park & Ride Buses** – A convenient way to avoid city-centre traffic and parking hassles.

Main Bus Routes for Tourists

- **Durham Cathedral Bus (No. 40 & 40A)** – If you don't want to walk up the hill to **Durham Cathedral**, this bus takes you straight to the doorstep.
- **X12 (Durham to Newcastle)** – A scenic ride to **Newcastle**, stopping at Durham University and the Angel of the North.
- **6, 7, 8 (Durham to Bishop Auckland & Barnard Castle)** – Perfect if you want to explore **Auckland Castle** or take a countryside trip.

Bus Ticket Prices & Tips

- A **single ticket** costs around **£2.50**.
- A **day ticket** for unlimited travel is around **£5.50**.
- Contactless payments are available on most buses.

- **Use the "Go North East" app** to check real-time bus arrivals.

Taxis: Quick & Reliable Transport

Durham's taxi services are widely available and great for short journeys, especially late at night when buses are less frequent.

Popular Taxi Companies

- **Mac's Taxis** – One of the most reputable and available 24/7.
- **JD's Taxis** – Offers competitive pricing and larger vehicles.
- **PRC Taxis** – Known for fast response times.

Estimated Taxi Fares

- Durham Train Station to City Centre: **£5-£8**
- Durham Cathedral to Durham University: **£6-£10**
- Durham to Newcastle: **£35-£45**

Taxi Tip: Taxis can be pre-booked or found at designated ranks, but they don't always accept card payments, so keep some cash handy.

Ride-Sharing: Uber & Local Alternatives

Uber operates in Durham, but availability can be limited, especially late at night. If Uber is unavailable, you can use local ride-hailing apps such as:

- **Bolt** – A popular alternative with competitive prices.
- **Amber Cars** – A local ride-sharing service.

Walking & Cycling

Walking: The Best Way to See Durham

Durham is a **walker's paradise**. With its medieval cobbled streets, breathtaking river views, and hidden alleyways, walking allows you to take in the beauty of the city at your own pace.

Best Walking Routes in Durham

1. **Durham Heritage Walk (1.5 miles)**
   - Start at **Durham Market Place**.
   - Walk up to **Durham Cathedral and Castle**, taking in the stunning architecture.

- Stroll down **Prebends Bridge** for one of the most iconic views of the River Wear.
2. **River Wear Circular Walk (2.5 miles)**
   - A peaceful riverside trail with spectacular views of Durham Cathedral.
   - Passes through **Pelaw Woods**, perfect for nature lovers.
3. **Botanic Garden Trail (1.8 miles)**
   - Wander through the **Durham University Botanic Garden**.
   - Ideal for plant lovers and those wanting a relaxing escape from the city.

Cycling: A Fun & Green Way to Travel

Durham is **bike-friendly**, with designated cycle paths and scenic countryside routes.

Best Cycling Routes

1. **Durham City Loop (5 miles)** – A gentle loop around the city centre, including the riverbanks.
2. **Durham to Sunderland Cycle Path (12 miles)** – A scenic ride following the old railway line.

3. **The Lanchester Valley Railway Path (13 miles)** – A beautiful countryside ride along a former railway.

Bike Rentals in Durham

- **The Cycle Hub** – Offers daily rentals starting from **£10 per day**.
- **Durham Bikes** – Electric and standard bike rentals available.

Cycling Tip: Durham is **hilly**, so if you're not an experienced cyclist, consider renting an **electric bike**!

Car Rentals & Parking: Where to Park & Drive in Durham

Renting a Car in Durham

While Durham's compact size means you don't need a car to get around the city, renting one is useful if you plan to explore **the Durham Dales, Beamish Museum, or the North Pennines**.

Best Car Rental Companies in Durham

- **Enterprise Rent-A-Car** – Located in the city centre and at Newcastle Airport.

- **Hertz Durham** – Offers a range of vehicles, including electric cars.
- **Europcar Durham** – Good deals on long-term rentals.

Parking in Durham: Where to Leave Your Car

Durham's historic streets make city-centre parking limited, but there are plenty of options outside the core area.

Best Parking Areas

1. **Prince Bishops Car Park** – Central location, ideal for shopping & dining.
2. **Durham Park & Ride** – Located outside the city to avoid traffic.
3. **Riverwalk Car Park** – Close to bars, restaurants, and the cinema.

Parking Fees

- City Centre Parking: **£1.50 - £2.50 per hour**.
- Park & Ride: **£2 per day** (includes unlimited bus travel).

Driving Tip: Avoid driving in the historic city centre during peak hours, as the narrow streets can get congested.

Accessibility for Travelers: Facilities for Visitors with Disabilities

Durham is working hard to be **inclusive and accessible**, ensuring that visitors with disabilities have an enjoyable and stress-free experience.

Public Transport Accessibility

- **Buses:** All Durham buses are **low-floor and wheelchair-accessible**.
- **Taxis:** Most major taxi services offer **wheelchair-accessible vehicles**.
- **Trains:** Durham Train Station has step-free access, elevators, and assistance services.

Accessible Attractions in Durham

- **Durham Cathedral** – Offers **ramped access** and **wheelchair-friendly tours**.
- **Durham Castle** – While the castle has some steep areas, **guided accessible tours** are available.

- **Gala Theatre & Cinema** – Has **hearing loops, wheelchair spaces, and accessible restrooms**.

Hotels & Accommodations with Accessible Rooms

1. **Radisson Blu Hotel** – Features wheelchair-friendly rooms and step-free entrances.
2. **Hotel Indigo Durham** – Offers spacious accessible rooms and lift access.
3. **Premier Inn Durham City Centre** – Budget-friendly and fully accessible.

Accessibility Tip: Durham has **free mobility scooter hire** available at the **MarketPlace** for visitors who need assistance.

Final Thoughts

Durham is a wonderfully **walkable and well-connected** city, offering a variety of ways to get around that suit every traveler's needs. Whether you prefer **public transport, cycling, or exploring on foot**, you'll find that Durham's compact layout makes travel easy and enjoyable.

Now that you know how to navigate Durham like a pro, let's move on to **where to stay in Durham**

Where to Stay in Durham

Durham, with its rich history, scenic beauty, and welcoming atmosphere, offers a range of accommodation options that will make your stay truly memorable. Whether you're seeking the **luxury** of a **5-star hotel**, the charm of a **boutique inn**, or the comfort of a **self-catering cottage**, Durham has something for everyone. Let's take a look at the best places to stay, ensuring that you feel right at home, no matter your budget or preferences.

Luxury Hotels & Boutique Stays – 5-Star Comfort & Unique Accommodations

For those who want to immerse themselves in absolute luxury and experience Durham at its finest, the city boasts a selection of **5-star hotels** and **boutique stays** that promise nothing short of **comfort, elegance, and style**. These accommodations not only provide exceptional service but are also designed to make your time in Durham an unforgettable experience.

Lumley Castle Hotel

Step back in time at the majestic **Lumley Castle Hotel**, where you'll stay in a beautifully restored medieval castle surrounded by acres of parkland. This **luxurious retreat** offers the rare opportunity to experience living in a **historic castle** while enjoying all the modern amenities you could desire. Imagine waking up in an elegant, **spacious room**, where **sumptuous furnishings** and **castle-inspired décor** transport you to another era. The **on-site restaurant** serves delicious local and seasonal dishes, perfect after a day of exploring Durham's attractions. A stay here promises an unforgettable blend of **history**, **luxury**, and **comfort**.

Hotel Indigo Durham

Located just steps from Durham Cathedral, **Hotel Indigo** is a **boutique gem** offering contemporary luxury with a **stylish twist**. The hotel's vibrant interiors, inspired by Durham's industrial past, perfectly combine modern design with historical touches. From **sleek, modern rooms** featuring soft linens and stylish furnishings to a top-floor **rooftop bar** offering **stunning views** of the cathedral, this hotel makes every moment of your stay special. **Personalized service** and a chic ambiance make it the ideal destination for those seeking both **luxury** and a **unique experience**.

The Finchale Abbey

For something truly extraordinary, stay at the **Finchale Abbey**, a **boutique hotel** set in the **ruins of a 13th-century abbey**. As you enter the abbey's grounds, you'll be greeted by stunning views and a **peaceful atmosphere**, making it feel like an idyllic sanctuary. The rooms, decorated with a tasteful mix of modern comforts and historic charm, offer a tranquil retreat after a day of exploration. Breakfast on the patio, overlooking the peaceful abbey, is the perfect start to any day.

Budget-Friendly Accommodation & Hostels – Affordable & Convenient Options

For those who prefer to explore Durham on a budget, don't worry—there are plenty of **affordable and convenient accommodation options** that will allow you to experience all the beauty and charm of this historic city without breaking the bank. Whether you're traveling solo or with a group, these stays offer great value without sacrificing comfort.

YHA Durham

Located within walking distance of Durham City Centre, **YHA Durham** offers a perfect combination of **budget-friendly accommodation** and **convenient location**. The **modern rooms** are simple but comfortable, and with a range of **shared dorms** and **private rooms**, it's ideal for travelers of all kinds. After a day of sightseeing, relax in the cozy lounge area or take advantage of the **self-catering kitchen**. Whether you're traveling on your own or with friends, YHA Durham is an excellent choice for those who want to enjoy the city's best attractions without spending a fortune.

Durham Castle Hostel

For a truly **unique and affordable experience**, stay at **Durham Castle Hostel**, where you can spend the night in a **room within the castle walls** itself! Offering simple, comfortable, and affordable rooms, the castle hostel gives you the chance to experience the **history and grandeur** of Durham Castle without the hefty price tag. Imagine spending your night in a **medieval setting**, surrounded by centuries of history. Whether you choose a **shared dorm** or a **private room**, staying at the castle hostel is a memory you'll treasure forever.

The Durham Marriott Hotel

A **budget-friendly option** with plenty of amenities is **The Durham Marriott Hotel**. Located just outside the city center, this hotel offers a range of comfortable rooms, perfect for visitors who prefer the convenience of modern facilities at a **great price**. With an **on-site restaurant**, **fitness center**, and **indoor pool**, you'll have everything you need for a comfortable stay. Plus, it's just a short bus ride from Durham's top attractions, making it an excellent base for exploring.

Family-Friendly Stays & Self-Catering Cottages

For families or groups of friends traveling together, Durham offers a range of **spacious and comfortable accommodations** that cater to everyone's needs. From **self-catering cottages** to family-friendly hotels, you'll find the perfect place to stay while enjoying the city's attractions together.

Durham Riverside Apartments

If you're looking for a **home-away-from-home** experience, consider booking a stay at **Durham Riverside Apartments**. These **self-catering apartments** are ideal for families, providing plenty of space for everyone to spread out and enjoy their stay. With **fully equipped kitchens**, you can prepare your own meals and enjoy them in the comfort of your private living room. The **riverfront location** offers stunning views, and the apartments are just a short walk from the city center, making it easy to explore Durham's best attractions.

The Old Post Office

For something a little more unique, book a stay at **The Old Post Office**, a charming self-catering cottage located just outside of Durham. This **converted historical building** offers plenty of space for families or groups, with **three cozy bedrooms**, a **fully equipped kitchen**, and a welcoming living area. Relax on the **private garden patio** or take a walk to explore the surrounding countryside. The peaceful setting and modern amenities make this cottage the perfect spot for families seeking comfort and relaxation.

The Bell Guest House

For families who enjoy staying in **bed-and-breakfast** accommodations, **The Bell Guest House** is a charming, family-friendly option. Situated in the heart of Durham, this welcoming guest house offers a selection of family rooms, complete with **modern amenities** and the perfect **homey atmosphere** for a good night's rest. The friendly staff goes above and beyond to ensure you and your little ones feel comfortable, and the **full English breakfast** served each morning is the perfect way to start your day of exploring.

Unique Stays – Castles, Manor Houses & Historic Inns

For those looking for something truly **extraordinary**, Durham offers several **unique accommodations** that will transport you back in time. Whether you're sleeping in the **shadow of a castle**, staying in a **manor house**, or spending the night in a **historic inn**, these accommodations will make your stay in Durham feel like a fairy tale.

Barnard Castle – The Kings Head Hotel

Step into history with a stay at **The Kings Head Hotel** in nearby Barnard Castle. This historic inn offers a **distinctly British experience**, where you can unwind in the comfort of its charming rooms, enjoy locally sourced food, and sip a drink by the fire in the **traditional pub**. Located near the **Barnard Castle**, you'll find yourself surrounded by **natural beauty** and **historic intrigue**. This is a perfect spot for those looking for both **charm** and **character** in their accommodation.

The Chester Moor House

For a true **taste of elegance**, stay in the **Chester Moor House**, a **luxurious manor house** just outside Durham. Set in sprawling grounds, this stunning property offers refined rooms with **stunning views** over the countryside. The house's rich **period features** blend seamlessly with modern comforts, making it the perfect choice for anyone seeking a memorable, **classical experience** in Durham. After a day of exploring, relax in the **elegant lounge** with a glass of wine and enjoy the serene atmosphere of this beautiful property.

The Lord Crewe Arms

For a **historic inn** experience with a twist, stay at **The Lord Crewe Arms** in the **village of Blanchland**, just outside Durham. This historic pub offers a welcoming atmosphere, traditional rooms, and hearty meals. What makes this inn unique is its location: surrounded by **rolling hills** and **picturesque landscapes**, it's the ideal place for those who want to experience **history** and **nature** together. Whether you're hiking the nearby trails or enjoying a warm drink by the fire, the inn provides a **comfortable and memorable** place to stay.

Whether you're looking for **5-star luxury**, a **budget-friendly hostel**, or a **charming manor house** steeped in history, Durham offers a wide variety of **accommodation options** that will make your stay as memorable as the city itself. From the moment you arrive, you'll feel welcomed, comfortable, and ready to explore all that Durham has to offer. With so many **unique stays** and **comfortable options**, it's easy to find the perfect place to rest your head after a day of discovery.

Top Must-See Attractions in Durham

Durham is a city where history whispers from the medieval stone walls, where the River Wear curves gracefully around a skyline dominated by ancient towers, and where every cobbled street has a story to tell. Whether you're drawn to the grandeur of Durham Cathedral, the medieval might of Durham Castle, or the tranquility of its lush gardens, this city offers something for every traveler.

In this chapter, we'll explore Durham's **must-see attractions**, each a gem in its own right, offering a mix of history, culture, and natural beauty.

Durham Cathedral – The Jewel of the City

Imagine standing before a masterpiece that has stood for almost a thousand years, its towering sandstone walls reaching toward the heavens. Durham Cathedral isn't just a building; it's **an experience**—a breathtaking encounter with medieval architecture, spiritual serenity, and a sense of timelessness that lingers long after you leave.

Built in **1093**, this UNESCO World Heritage Site is considered **one of the greatest Norman structures in Europe**. Its grand, rib-vaulted ceilings, stained-glass windows, and intricate stonework make it a marvel of medieval craftsmanship. But Durham Cathedral is more than a historic monument—it remains a **living place of worship** and a vibrant cultural hub.

Must-See Highlights Inside the Cathedral

- **The Nave:** Step inside and be awed by the sheer scale of the cathedral's interior, with its enormous columns, delicate stone carvings, and the play of light through stained glass.
- **The Shrine of St. Cuthbert:** Pilgrims have traveled here for centuries to pay their respects to the saint whose remains rest within this sacred space.
- **The Galilee Chapel:** Home to the tomb of **The Venerable Bede**, one of medieval England's greatest scholars.
- **The Tower:** Climb **325 steps** for a panoramic view of Durham's rooftops, the River Wear, and the surrounding countryside.

Tours & Special Events

- **Guided Tours:** Learn the cathedral's fascinating history from knowledgeable guides.
- **Stained Glass Workshops:** Try your hand at an ancient craft and create your own masterpiece.
- **Christmas at the Cathedral:** Experience the magic of candlelit carol services in December.

Durham Castle – A Norman Fortress & UNESCO World Heritage Site

A Castle of Conquerors, Scholars & Royalty

Perched high above the city, **Durham Castle** has stood as a guardian of the River Wear for over **900 years**. Built by **William the Conqueror** in 1072, it was originally a military stronghold before becoming the seat of the powerful **Prince-Bishops of Durham**.

Today, the castle serves as a **student residence** for Durham University, making it one of the few **inhabited castles** in the UK.

But don't worry—you don't need to enroll in a course to explore its historic halls!

What to See at Durham Castle

- **The Great Hall:** A grand medieval dining space that still hosts student feasts today.
- **The Norman Chapel:** The oldest surviving part of the castle, adorned with exquisite **Romanesque carvings**.
- **The Keep:** Once a fortress, now student accommodation—but still worth admiring from the outside!
- **The Castle Courtyard:** A peaceful spot with incredible views of the cathedral.

How to Visit

- **Guided Tours Only:** Due to its role as a university building, the castle is only accessible via guided tours, which provide a rare glimpse into its past.
- **Photography Tip:** Stand in **Palace Green** for the best view of **Durham Cathedral & Castle together**—one of England's most iconic sights.

Palace Green Library – A Treasure Trove of Knowledge

Tucked between **Durham Cathedral and Durham Castle**, **Palace Green Library** is a hidden treasure trove of rare books, historic manuscripts, and fascinating exhibitions. While it may not have the towering grandeur of its UNESCO-listed neighbors, this library holds something just as magical: **centuries of knowledge**.

Highlights of Palace Green Library

- **The Bishop Cosin's Library:** A **17th-century reading room** that looks like something out of a Harry Potter film, complete with antique wooden shelves and centuries-old books.
- **The Archives of Durham University:** Home to some of the most important **medieval manuscripts** and **local history records** in England.
- **The Changing Exhibitions:** Featuring everything from **ancient maps of Durham** to **artifacts from Egypt**.

Why You Should Visit

- It's a quiet escape from the busy streets, perfect for book lovers and history buffs.
- It offers **free exhibitions**, making it an excellent budget-friendly attraction.
- You'll get to see rare manuscripts **not found anywhere else in the world.**

Botanic Garden – Exotic Plants & Serene Walks

A Natural Wonderland in the Heart of Durham

If you need a break from history and architecture, **Durham University Botanic Garden** offers a breath of fresh air. Spread across **10 hectares**, this garden is home to **exotic plants**, **tranquil walking trails**, and **hidden sculptures**, making it a perfect spot for relaxation and exploration.

Things to See & Do at the Botanic Garden

- **Glasshouse Collection:** Step into a **tropical rainforest** and see exotic orchids, banana trees, and carnivorous plants.

- **Woodland Walks:** Wander through the shaded paths, where you might spot **red squirrels** and rare birds.
- **Sculpture Trail:** Look out for art pieces hidden among the greenery.
- **Seasonal Highlights:**
    - **Spring:** Bluebells carpet the woodlands.
    - **Summer:** The **wildflower meadow** bursts into color.
    - **Autumn:** Japanese maples turn fiery red.
    - **Winter:** Snow-covered trees create a magical atmosphere.

Why It's Worth Visiting

- A great place for **nature photography**.
- Perfect for families—kids love the **interactive discovery zone**.
- A peaceful retreat just **a short walk from the city centre**.

Durham University Museum of Archaeology – A Journey Through Time

Located inside **Palace Green Library**, **Durham University Museum of**

Archaeology is a small but fascinating museum that takes you on a journey through Durham's prehistoric, Roman, and medieval past.

What to See at the Museum

- **Prehistoric Artifacts:** Tools and pottery from Durham's earliest settlers.
- **Roman Remains:** Including coins, jewelry, and everyday objects found in excavations.
- **Medieval Durham Exhibits:** Get a glimpse of life in the **Middle Ages**, from knights to common folk.
- **The Viking Connection:** Evidence of Viking raids and Norse influence in Northern England.

Interactive Exhibits & Hands-On Activities

- Try your hand at **Roman pottery making**.
- Handle **real artifacts** under the guidance of museum staff.
- Join a **medieval reenactment event** in summer!

Why You Should Visit

- It's **free to enter**, making it a fantastic **budget-friendly** attraction.
- Great for **history enthusiasts** and **families with kids**.
- It offers a different perspective of Durham's past beyond its famous castle and cathedral.

Final Thoughts

Durham's **must-see attractions** offer a perfect blend of history, culture, and natural beauty. Whether you're exploring the magnificent **Durham Cathedral**, stepping into the medieval world of **Durham Castle**, or immersing yourself in rare books at **Palace Green Library**, this city invites you to **discover something new at every turn**.

Next, let's dive into **Durham's hidden gems—lesser-known but equally fascinating places waiting to be explored!**

Hidden Gems & Off-the-Beaten-Path Attractions in Durham

Durham may be famous for its awe-inspiring cathedral and commanding medieval castle, but beyond these well-known landmarks lies a world of hidden treasures. These places are **tucked away from the tourist trail**, waiting to be discovered by those with a curious spirit and a sense of adventure. Some are **mystical ruins cloaked in history**, others are **secret gardens bursting with life**, and a few are **places where time seems to stand still**, offering a glimpse into Durham's lesser-known past.

This chapter is for **explorers**, for those who crave **mystery**, and for travelers who want to **uncover the unexpected**. If you're ready to step off the beaten path, Durham has plenty to reveal.

Finchale Priory — A Riverside Medieval Ruin

Just four miles from the bustling streets of Durham lies **Finchale Priory**, a breathtaking medieval ruin **nestled beside the River**

Wear. Once a place of devotion and quiet contemplation, today it stands as a hauntingly beautiful reminder of a bygone era. The priory is **enveloped in legends**, its stones whispering tales of monks, miracles, and mystery.

The Story of Finchale Priory

The priory was founded in **1196** on the site of the hermitage of **St. Godric**, a sailor-turned-holy-man who spent decades here in solitude, living among the forests and wild animals. After his death, his sanctuary became a Benedictine monastery, housing monks who sought a peaceful retreat from their lives at Durham Cathedral.

But Finchale's peace was not eternal. With the dissolution of the monasteries under **King Henry VIII**, it fell into ruin, its once-grand halls left to the mercy of nature. Today, ivy creeps through ancient archways, and the **weathered stone walls glow golden in the afternoon light**, creating an eerie yet magical atmosphere.

What to Explore at Finchale Priory

- **The Main Church Ruins** – Walk through towering archways and **imagine the monks chanting centuries ago**.
- **The Riverbank Trails** – Follow the winding **woodland paths**, where **St. Godric himself once walked in solitude**.
- **The Hidden Crypt** – A dimly lit chamber that once held sacred relics—can you feel its mysterious presence?
- **The Old Bridge Over the Wear** – A perfect **photo spot** that frames the priory beautifully.

Local Tip: Visit at **sunset** when the ruins are bathed in golden light—it's a sight straight out of a fantasy novel.

The Oriental Museum – A Collection of Asian Treasures

Did you know that **Durham is home to one of the finest collections of Asian artifacts in the UK?** Tucked away in a quiet corner of Durham University, **The Oriental Museum** feels like stepping into another world—one filled with **ancient Chinese scrolls,**

Egyptian mummies, and dazzling Persian ceramics.

What You'll Discover

- **Egyptian Mummies & Tomb Artifacts** – See a **real sarcophagus** and learn about ancient burial customs.
- **Imperial Chinese Treasures** – Delicate **jade carvings, intricate silk robes, and ancient calligraphy scrolls**.
- **Middle Eastern Art & Ceramics** – Stunning Islamic **tiles, pottery, and manuscripts** from Persia and beyond.
- **Samurai Armor & Japanese Swords** – A glimpse into the world of Japan's **legendary warriors**.

This **hidden museum** is a paradise for **history lovers**, yet it remains **one of Durham's best-kept secrets**.

Why Visit?

- **Perfect for a rainy day** in Durham.
- **Small but packed with treasures**, making it easy to explore in an hour or two.

- **Not crowded**, so you can admire the exhibits without distractions.

Wharton Park – Best Views Over Durham's Skyline

Want to see **the best panoramic view of Durham**? Head to **Wharton Park**, a stunning green space that sits **on a hill overlooking the city**, offering breathtaking vistas of **Durham Cathedral, the Castle, and the River Wear**.

What to See & Do at Wharton Park

- **The Best View of Durham** – Stand at the **viewing platform** and take in the entire skyline—it's postcard-perfect!
- **Secret Gardens & Winding Paths** – Explore **hidden flower gardens, wild woodlands, and peaceful benches** where you can sit and soak in the scenery.
- **Historic Railway Connections** – Learn about Durham's role in **railway history**, as this park once **overlooked the world's first passenger railway station**.

- **A Great Spot for a Picnic** – Bring some local treats and **enjoy lunch with a view**.

Insider Tip: Visit **at sunrise** for a truly magical moment—the cathedral glowing in soft golden light is something you'll never forget.

Old Durham Gardens

Most visitors to Durham never hear about **Old Durham Gardens**, a **secluded 17th-century garden** tucked away just outside the city. With its **manicured terraces, stone staircases, and blooming orchards**, this garden feels like a place frozen in time—a peaceful sanctuary away from the crowds.

What Makes It Special?

- **Terraced Flower Gardens** – A **picturesque escape**, perfect for a quiet afternoon walk.
- **Historic Orchard** – Home to ancient **apple and pear trees**, with fruit ripening in late summer.
- **Stone Pavilion & Fountain** – A charming architectural gem hidden among the greenery.

Unlike Durham's **busier parks**, Old Durham Gardens remains **a local secret**. If you're looking for **peace, beauty, and a touch of history**, this is the place to go.

Durham's Underground Pubs & Historic Alehouses – Unique Drinking Spots

Durham's cobbled streets and medieval alleyways **hide some of the most atmospheric pubs in England**—places where monks once **brewed their own ale**, smugglers **plotted secret deals**, and where Durham's rich **pub culture** still thrives today.

Must-Visit Pubs & Historic Alehouses

The Dun Cow – The Ghostly Tavern

- A **300-year-old pub is said** to be haunted by the spirit of a **mysterious woman**.
- Cozy fireplaces, **old wooden beams**, and a fantastic selection of real ales.

The Shakespeare Tavern – Durham's Oldest Pub

- **Dating back to 1190**, this **medieval alehouse** once served monks from Durham Cathedral.
- Expect **oak-paneled walls, candlelit corners, and traditional English cask ales**.

The Victoria Inn – A Victorian Time Capsule

- A **tiny, unchanged pub from the 1800s**, complete with **gas lamps and antique decor**.
- A favorite spot for **Durham locals**—if you love an authentic, no-frills pub, this is it.

The Cellar Door – A Bar in an Underground Vault

- **Tucked beneath a medieval street**, this modern cocktail bar sits inside an **old stone cellar**.
- Try a **local gin cocktail** while soaking in the **historic atmosphere**.

Final Thoughts: The Secret Side of Durham

These **hidden gems** prove that **Durham is full of surprises**. Whether you're **exploring medieval ruins, discovering treasures from the East, gazing over the city's skyline, or sipping ale in a centuries-old tavern**, there's always **something new and unexpected** to uncover.

For those who seek **mystery, adventure, and a deeper connection to Durham's past**, these places are waiting to be explored. **The question is—where will you go first?**

The Best Things to Do in Durham

Durham is **more than just a historic city**—it's a **living, breathing adventure**, waiting to be explored. From **gliding along the River Wear** in a kayak to **strolling through centuries-old markets**, from **ghostly encounters in ancient alleyways** to **theatrical performances in a grand venue**, Durham offers **something for every kind of traveler**.

This city **blends old and new seamlessly**—you can **uncover medieval mysteries by day and enjoy a vibrant performance at night**. Whether you prefer **thrilling outdoor adventures, cultural experiences, or simply soaking in the city's timeless beauty**, this chapter will guide you through Durham's **top experiences**.

So, **are you ready to dive in?** Here's what you absolutely **must do** when visiting Durham!

River Wear Boat Tours & Kayaking Adventures

See Durham from the Water

There's something truly **magical** about floating down the **River Wear**, surrounded by **lush green landscapes**, with **Durham Cathedral and Castle towering above you**. The river **curves around the city**, offering some of the **most spectacular views** you can find.

Ways to Explore the River Wear

- **Boat Tours** – Sit back, relax, and **let an expert guide** take you through Durham's fascinating history.
- **Kayaking & Canoeing** – For an **active adventure**, paddle along the river and discover **hidden corners of Durham**.
- **Punting** – Try your hand at this **classic English boating tradition**—it's a peaceful and romantic way to experience Durham's waterways.

Best River Experiences in Durham

Durham City Boat Club Tours

- **A leisurely cruise past Durham's most famous landmarks.**

- Learn about the **city's history from a knowledgeable guide**.
- **Perfect for families** and those who want to relax while taking in the sights.

Wear Kayak Adventures

- **Paddle your own kayak or canoe** for a more immersive experience.
- Explore **secluded riverbanks and hidden wildlife spots**.
- **Great for adventure seekers**—be ready to get a little wet!

Sunset Punting on the Wear

- **A dreamy, romantic experience**, perfect for couples.
- Watch the sunset **over the medieval skyline** as you float gently down the river.

Insider Tip: If you're visiting **in autumn**, the trees lining the riverbanks turn **a dazzling mix of gold, orange, and red**, making the experience **even more breathtaking**.

Ghost Walks & Haunted History Tours

Durham's Darker Side

Durham is **a city of legends**, with **centuries-old alleyways, eerie ruins, and stories of ghosts that still linger**. If you love **mystery and spine-tingling tales**, then a **ghost tour** is a must.

What to Expect on a Ghost Tour

- **Hear chilling stories of haunted buildings**, restless spirits, and strange happenings.
- **Visit erie locations**, including **shadowy passageways, graveyards, and historic inns**.
- **Feel the atmosphere** as expert storytellers bring **Durham's ghostly past to life**.

Best Ghost Tours in Durham

Durham Ghost Walks

- **Led by expert guides**, this tour takes you through **some of the city's most haunted spots**.
- Learn about **The Grey Lady of Durham Castle**, the **mysterious monk of the Cathedral**, and other restless spirits.

The Hidden Durham Tour

- A mix of **local folklore and secret historical stories**.
- Explore parts of Durham **most visitors never see**.

The Shadowy Streets Experience

- A nighttime tour through Durham's **old alleyways and forgotten corners**.
- Expect **a few surprises along the way!**

Dare to take a ghost tour? Even if you're a skeptic, these **eerie stories will stay with you long after the night ends**.

Shopping at Durham Indoor Market

Durham Indoor Market is **not your average shopping center**—it's a **bustling, old-world marketplace**, filled with **independent traders, handcrafted goods, and fresh local produce**. Whether you're looking for **unique souvenirs, gourmet treats, or vintage treasures**, this place **has it all**.

What You'll Find in the Market

- **Handmade Jewelry & Crafts** – Meet local artisans and find **one-of-a-kind gifts**.
- **Fresh Produce & Gourmet Foods** – From **homemade cheeses to traditional English pies**.
- **Rare Books & Antiques** – If you love history, you'll find **old maps, rare prints, and classic novels**.

Why Visit?

- **Authentic, local shopping experience.**
- **Great place to chat with friendly Durham locals.**
- **Delicious street food stalls**—try a traditional **stottie cake** or **handmade fudge**.

Exploring Durham's Iconic Bridges & Riverside Walks

Scenic Walks with Stunning Views

Durham is **a city built around water**, and its **bridges and riverside walks** offer some of the **most breathtaking views**. Whether you're up for a **long scenic stroll** or just want a **quiet moment by the river**, these spots are perfect.

Must-See Bridges in Durham

Prebends Bridge

- The most **picturesque bridge** in Durham.
- **Best viewpoint of Durham Cathedral towering above the river**.

Elvet Bridge

- A **historic stone bridge** with **hidden medieval vaults underneath**.
- **Perfect for sunset photography.**

Framwellgate Bridge

- One of the **oldest bridges in Durham**, dating back to the **12th century**.
- Cross it and you'll find **charming cafes and boutique shops nearby**.

Best Riverside Walks

- **The Durham River Walk – A peaceful route along the banks of the Wear**, offering stunning views.
- **The Woodland Trail** – A more **secluded walk through lush greenery and hidden paths**.

Local Tip: Visit **early in the morning** for a truly **magical, quiet experience**—the mist rising over the river is something straight out of a fairy tale.

Attending a Performance at Gala Theatre & Cinema

For those who love **theatre, live music, and film**, a visit to **Gala Theatre & Cinema** is a must. This **modern venue** hosts **a variety of performances**, from **Shakespearean plays to stand-up comedy and music concerts**.

What's On?

- **West End-style performances**
- **Indie film screenings**
- **Comedy nights** featuring top UK comedians
- **Live music performances** across different genres

Why Visit?

- **Great way to experience local culture**.
- **Perfect for a relaxing evening after a day of exploring**.

Local Tip: Check their schedule **in advance**, as special **seasonal performances** sell out quickly!

Visiting the Durham World Heritage Visitor Centre

Want to **truly understand** what makes Durham **so special**? The **Durham World Heritage Visitor Centre** is the best place to start.

What You'll Learn

- **The history of Durham Cathedral & Castle**—why they're **UNESCO-protected**.
- **The city's medieval origins** and its role in **shaping England's religious history**.
- **Interactive exhibits & displays**, bringing **Durham's past to life**.

Why Go?

- **Perfect for history lovers.**
- **Gives context to the landmarks you'll explore in Durham.**

Final Thoughts: Durham Awaits!

Durham is a city **overflowing with adventure**. Whether you want to **explore the river, experience ghostly thrills, shop for hidden treasures, or enjoy a cultural night out**, there's **never a dull moment**.

Best Day Trips from Durham

Durham is a city rich in **history, charm, and adventure**, but one of its greatest advantages is its **proximity to incredible day-trip destinations**. Within an hour's journey, you can find yourself **walking through a Victorian-era town, gazing at a dramatic waterfall, hunting for fossils on the coast, or exploring bustling cities** filled with culture.

Whether you're a **history buff, nature enthusiast, art lover, or explorer at heart**, these **five unforgettable day trips** will add **even more magic** to your time in Durham.

So, **pack your sense of adventure**—and let's hit the road!

Beamish Museum – Step Back in Time at This Living History Museum

Imagine stepping into a **time machine** and finding yourself in a **Victorian village, a 1940s farm, or an early 20th-century** mining town—this is exactly what **Beamish Museum** offers.

Set in **300 acres of stunning countryside**, Beamish is **one of the UK's most immersive living history museums**, where **history comes alive**. Here, you **don't just see the past—you live it**.

What Makes Beamish Special?

- **Costumed actors** bring history to life, from shopkeepers to miners.
- **Authentic buildings** and streets, moved brick-by-brick from their original locations.
- **Vintage trams and buses** transport you through different time periods.
- **Hands-on activities**—try baking in an Edwardian kitchen, making sweets in an old-fashioned sweet shop, or even riding a steam engine.

Top Highlights

The 1900s Town

- Stroll down **cobbled streets lined with period shops, a pub, a bank, and even a traditional sweet shop** where you can watch **boiled sweets being made the old-fashioned way.**

The 1940s Farm

- Experience **wartime Britain**, where families had to grow their own food, ration supplies, and **navigate the challenges of WWII life.**

The 1900s Pit Village & Colliery

- Step inside **a real coal mine**, see how miners worked, and **explore a traditional mining village schoolhouse and chapel.**

Beamish Tramway & Vintage Vehicles

- Ride a **restored Edwardian tram** or hop on a **1940s bus** to explore the vast museum grounds in style.

Getting There: Beamish Museum is **30 minutes by car from Durham**, with regular buses also available.

Barnard Castle & Bowes Museum

Nestled in the **Durham Dales, Barnard Castle** is a **charming market town** brimming with **history, independent shops, and scenic riverside views**. Its biggest attraction? **The ruins of Barnard Castle itself**, a **medieval fortress** with breathtaking views over the **River Tees**.

The Castle's Mystical Past

- Built in the **12th century** by the powerful **Balliol family**.
- Later owned by **Richard III**, the controversial King of England.
- Offers **panoramic views** of the countryside—bring your camera!

Bowes Museum – A French Château in England

Just a short walk from the castle, the **Bowes Museum** is **a world-class art gallery housed in a magnificent 19th-century French-style château**.

- Home to **over 30,000 pieces of art, furniture, and fashion**.
- Features works by **Goya, El Greco, and Canaletto**.
- Don't miss the **Silver Swan**, a mesmerizing **18th-century**

automaton that moves with clockwork precision.

Getting There: Barnard Castle is **40 minutes from Durham by car**.

High Force Waterfall & the Durham Dales

If you're craving **wild landscapes and jaw-dropping natural beauty**, a trip to **High Force Waterfall** in the **Durham Dales** is a must.

Here, the **River Tees plunges 21 meters (70 feet) over rugged rock formations**, creating one of **England's most powerful and stunning waterfalls**.

Why You'll Love High Force

- **Awe-inspiring views**—especially after heavy rainfall!
- **A scenic woodland walk** to reach the falls.
- **Great picnic spots** along the river.
- **Wildlife sightings**—look out for otters, red squirrels, and kingfishers.

The Durham Dales: Rolling Hills & Hidden Villages

After visiting High Force, take a drive through the **Durham Dales**, a landscape of **rolling green hills, charming stone villages, and winding country roads**.

Top Stops in the Dales:

- **Middleton-in-Teesdale** – A quaint village with tea rooms and riverside walks.
- **Eggleston Hall Gardens** – A hidden garden with **ancient trees, wildflowers, and a historic nursery**.

Getting There: High Force is **50 minutes from Durham by car**, with parking near the falls.

Seaham Beach & Coastal Walks – Fossil Hunting & Stunning Views

For **rugged cliffs, golden sands, and some of the best fossil hunting in the UK,** head to **Seaham Beach**.

Once a **Victorian seaside resort**, Seaham is now known for **its dramatic coastline, historic heritage, and hidden treasures**—including **seaglass** washed ashore from an old glass factory.

Top Things to Do in Seaham

Hunt for Sea Glass & Fossils

- Seaham's beach is **famous for colorful seaglass**, smoothed by the sea over decades.
- Keep an eye out for **fossilized coral and ancient ammonites**.

Walk Along the Durham Heritage Coast

- Follow the **clifftop paths** for stunning views over the North Sea.
- Stop at **Nose's Point**, a dramatic headland with breathtaking scenery.

Visit Seaham's Famous Tommy Statue

- This **9-foot-tall steel sculpture** is a moving tribute to WWI soldiers.

Getting There: Seaham is **25 minutes from Durham by car**.

Sunderland & Newcastle – Nearby City Escapes with Shopping & Culture

Just **30 minutes from Durham**, Sunderland offers **a mix of history, arts, and seaside charm**.

Best Things to Do in Sunderland

- **Roker & Seaburn Beaches** – Perfect for a **seaside walk or fish & chips**.
- **Sunderland Museum & Winter Gardens – Ancient fossils, local history, and lush botanical gardens under glass.**
- **The National Glass Centre** – Watch glassblowers create **beautiful handmade pieces**.

Newcastle – The Ultimate City Break

Lively, stylish, and full of energy, **Newcastle** is **just 15 minutes from Durham by train**.

Top Experiences in Newcastle

- **Stroll along the Quayside** – Iconic views of the **Tyne Bridge and Millennium Bridge**.
- **Explore the BALTIC Centre for Contemporary Art** – A world-renowned **modern art gallery**.

- **Visit the Castle Keep** – The **medieval origins of Newcastle**, dating back to the 12th century.
- **Enjoy shopping at Eldon Square & Grainger Market** – From **high-end brands to quirky independent shops**.

Final Thoughts: Adventure Beyond Durham Awaits!

Durham is a fantastic base for **exploring some of England's most exciting and diverse destinations**. Whether you want to **step into history at Beamish, marvel at a roaring waterfall, find hidden gems on the coast, or experience the buzz of Newcastle**, these day trips **will add adventure to your journey**.

Durham's Rich History & Culture

Durham is a city that **breathes history**. Walk through its **cobbled streets**, and you're treading the same paths as medieval monks, coal miners, and scholars who shaped not just the city but **the very fabric of England itself**.

Its **story is one of faith, resilience, and transformation**—from the arrival of **Saint Cuthbert's relics**, to the rise of **Durham's coal mining industry**, and its **enduring role as a seat of knowledge and learning**.

Let's journey through **Durham's fascinating past**, uncovering the moments and people that made this city **a beacon of heritage, tradition, and culture**.

Saint Cuthbert & The Lindisfarne Gospels

The Legend of Saint Cuthbert

To understand Durham's **spiritual heart**, we must begin with **Saint Cuthbert**, a 7th-century monk and hermit whose **miracles** and **devotion to faith** made him one of England's most revered saints.

Born in **Northumbria**, Cuthbert was drawn to a life of **solitude and prayer**, choosing to live in isolation on the **Holy Island of Lindisfarne**. He spent his days **preaching, healing the sick, and spreading Christianity across northern England**.

When he died in **687 AD**, he was buried at Lindisfarne. But his story **didn't end there**.

The Flight from Lindisfarne

In **793 AD**, the world changed. The **Vikings launched their first raid on England**, attacking Lindisfarne with terrifying force. The monks, fearing for the safety of **Cuthbert's remains**, fled the island, carrying his **coffin and relics**.

For over **a century**, they wandered through the North, searching for a place of refuge—until, finally, **they arrived in Durham in 995 AD**.

The Birth of Durham Cathedral

According to legend, when the monks reached Durham, they **could go no**

further—Cuthbert's coffin refused to move. Taking it as a divine sign, they established a **church on the hill**, where the magnificent **Durham Cathedral** now stands.

This cathedral became **a sacred pilgrimage site**, attracting thousands who sought **Cuthbert's blessings and miracles**.

The Lindisfarne Gospels – A Masterpiece of Faith & Art

During their journey, the monks also protected the **Lindisfarne Gospels**, a stunningly illuminated manuscript created in **the early 8th century**.

Even today, this masterpiece remains **one of the most treasured works of medieval art**, symbolizing **Durham's deep spiritual roots**.

Mining Heritage of County Durham – The Legacy of the Coal Industry

For centuries, **coal was the lifeblood of Durham**. Beneath its rolling hills lay **rich veins of coal**, and from the 18th to the 20th century, mining defined **life, work, and identity** in County Durham.

The Rise of the Coal Industry

By the **1700s**, coal mining was booming. **Durham's coal powered factories, fueled steam engines, and warmed homes across Britain**. Whole towns and villages grew around the **pits**, with generations of families working underground.

Miners formed **tight-knit communities**, bound by **hardship, shared struggles, and resilience**.

Life as a Durham Miner

A miner's life was **grueling**—descending into the **dark, narrow shafts** at dawn, working in **cramped, dangerous tunnels**, and emerging only after long, **backbreaking** shifts.

But beyond the hardship, there was **pride**. **Miners saw themselves as the backbone of Britain**, their labor **fueling the nation**.

The Legacy of the Durham Miners' Gala

Even today, Durham honors its mining past through the **Durham Miners' Gala**, a **vibrant annual event** that brings together former miners, families, and trade unions.

Held every July since **1871**, this **celebration of solidarity and tradition** fills the city with **music, banners, and a deep sense of heritage**.

Durham University: One of England's Oldest Institutions

Founded in **1832**, Durham University is **one of the oldest and most prestigious universities in England**. It was **the first university established after Oxford and Cambridge**, and its creation marked **a new chapter in British education**.

The Unique Collegiate System

Durham's structure is inspired by **Oxbridge**, with students belonging to **individual colleges**, each with its **own traditions, rivalries, and sense of identity**.

From the historic **University College (housed in Durham Castle!)** to the **modern Hill Colleges**, each plays a role in shaping the **lively academic and social scene**.

A Legacy of Academic Excellence

Durham has produced **world-renowned scholars, scientists, and writers**. Its departments—ranging from **theology to space physics**—are **globally respected**, and the university continues to be a **hub of learning, research, and discovery**.

With students from **over 150 countries**, Durham University is not just part of the city's history—it **is it's beating heart**.

Traditional Festivals & Local Events

Durham is a city that **loves to celebrate**. Throughout the year, its **ancient streets, historic squares, and riverside paths** come alive with **festivals, parades, and traditions** that have been passed down for generations.

The Durham Miners' Gala (The Big)Meeting

As mentioned earlier, the **Durham Miners' Gala** is one of the **largest working-class**

festivals in the world. Each July, thousands gather to **march through the city, carrying vibrant banners and playing brass band music**—a powerful tribute to Durham's mining past.

Durham Lumiere – A Dazzling Light Festival

Every two years, Durham hosts **Lumiere**, a breathtaking **festival of light and art**. The entire city is **transformed into an open-air gallery**, with **stunning light installations** illuminating Durham's streets, bridges, and cathedral.

The Durham Regatta – The Henley of the North

Dating back to **1834**, the **Durham Regatta** is one of **the oldest rowing events in the UK**. Every summer, the River Wear is filled with **competitive rowers**, thrilling races, and lively riverside celebrations.

Durham's Role in English History

Durham's history is a **tapestry woven with battles, betrayals, and power struggles**.

The Norman Conquest & the Prince Bishops

After the **Norman Conquest of 1066**, Durham became a stronghold of **Norman power**. The Normans built **Durham Castle** and granted its rulers—the **Prince Bishops of Durham**—unmatched authority.

These **Prince Bishops were like kings in their own right**, governing the region with **military, legal, and economic control**.

Battles & Revolts

Durham witnessed **many conflicts**, from **Viking raids** to the **Wars of the Roses**. It played a key role in the **English Civil War**, and its castle **imprisoned Scottish prisoners after the Battle of Dunbar (1650)**.

Durham Today – A City of Heritage & Innovation

Today, Durham is **a city that balances the old and the new**. While it **honors its medieval past**, it is also **a center of education, science, and the arts**.

From its **UNESCO-listed cathedral and castle** to its **world-class university and modern festivals**, Durham's legacy **continues to inspire**.

Final Thoughts: The Living History of Durham

Durham's **rich history is more than just dates and events**—it's a **story of faith, resilience, and transformation**. Whether through the **legend of Saint Cuthbert**, the **coal miners' legacy**, or the **prestige of Durham University**, this city is **a place where the past and present coexist beautifully**.

So, as you explore Durham, remember: **every street, every stone, and every tradition has a story to tell**.

Food & Drink in Durham

Nestled in the rolling hills of County Durham, this charming city is not only steeped in history but also brimming with **mouthwatering cuisine**. From hearty, **traditional dishes** that have been passed down through generations to contemporary fine dining experiences, Durham offers a **delicious tapestry of flavors** that will tantalize your taste buds and leave you craving more.

Whether you're sampling **local delicacies** in cozy cafés or sipping a cold pint in a centuries-old pub, the food and drink scene in Durham is an experience that will leave you hungry for another bite, another sip, and another memory. So, come and indulge in the **delicious flavors** of Durham, where every dish tells a story.

Must-Try Local Dishes — Traditional Foods of Durham

Durham's culinary history is rich and diverse, rooted in the **hearty, rustic flavors** of the North. The region has been shaped by centuries of farming, fishing, and mining, resulting in dishes that reflect both its **agricultural heritage** and the **coastal**

influence from the nearby North Sea. Here's a taste of what you must try while visiting:

Pease Pudding

This humble dish is an **iconic Durham favorite**, a comforting and **savory yellow split pea mash** that's been a staple for centuries. It's often served alongside **stott bread**, a thick, round, and slightly chewy flatbread—perfect for scooping up generous portions of pease pudding, or paired with a traditional **ham sandwich**. The **earthy flavor** of the peas, seasoned with **salt and pepper**, offers a satisfying, wholesome taste that's both filling and nostalgic.

Durham's Famous Sausages

There's no better way to experience Durham's culinary heart than through its sausages. **Durham sausages** are a **local specialty**, known for their **succulent, rich flavor**. Made with **locally sourced pork**, these sausages are seasoned with **herbs, spices, and a touch of sage**, giving them an aromatic kick. Often served with **mashed potatoes**, **gravy**, and a side of vegetables, they're perfect comfort food, offering the perfect balance of savory and rich flavors.

Fish and Chips

While fish and chips are beloved across the UK, the coastal influence of Durham means its version takes on a unique twist. Local fish, such as **cod** or **haddock**, is battered and deep-fried to a **crispy, golden perfection**, served alongside **crunchy, thick-cut fries**. Pair it with a **malt vinegar drizzle** or **tartar sauce**, and you'll get a truly authentic taste of Durham's culinary coast. Don't forget to add a **side of mushy peas**—a classic!

The Durham Pudding

End your meal with the **Durham pudding**, a luscious, **rich dessert** made from **suet, breadcrumbs, and golden syrup**. The result is a **sweet, sticky, and comforting treat** that's perfect for those cold, crisp evenings in Durham. Often paired with a dollop of fresh cream, this pudding is a reminder of Durham's **country-style cooking**—simple, satisfying, and full of flavor.

Best Pubs & Traditional Alehouses – Where to Drink Like a Local

No trip to Durham is complete without stepping into one of its **historic pubs** or alehouses, where the **local brewing culture** thrives and the **pints flow freely**. These iconic spots offer a warm welcome, cozy surroundings, and the opportunity to enjoy **local ales** that have been brewed right on Durham's doorstep. Here are a few of the best places to drink like a true Durham local:

The Dun Cow

A Durham institution, **The Dun Cow** is a **traditional pub** with a **rich history** and a vibrant atmosphere. Located in the heart of the city, this pub is **renowned for its selection of cask ales**, many of which are brewed locally by the **Durham Brewery**. The wooden beams, stone floors, and **rustic charm** make it the perfect place to cozy up with a pint of **Durham Magus**, a **rich, dark ale** with notes of **roasted malt** and **chocolate**. Pair it with a hearty meal from the menu, featuring **classic pub fare** such as **fish pie** and **beef and ale pie**, and you've got the perfect night out.

The Shakespeare Tavern

For a **more intimate experience**, head to **The Shakespeare Tavern**, one of the city's oldest alehouses. Nestled on the edge of the **market square**, this pub has a delightful,

old-world charm, with exposed brick walls and vintage portraits hanging from the walls. The menu here offers a range of **locally brewed ales**, including a refreshing **Durham Pale Ale**, which pairs beautifully with the tavern's **local cheeses** and **charcuterie boards**. It's the kind of place where you can spend hours **chatting with friends** over a pint, soaking in the historical ambiance.

The Kingslodge Inn

For those seeking a **more rustic experience**, **The Kingslodge Inn** offers a charming and cozy setting in the Durham countryside. With its welcoming atmosphere and **fantastic beer garden**, it's a great spot to enjoy a **summer afternoon pint**. Their **house ale** is a local favorite, and the **craft beer selection** is constantly changing, showcasing the best of **Durham's brewing scene**. Be sure to sample the **Durham Brewery's Black Bob Ale**, a **smooth, slightly hoppy** beer with a hint of **roastiness**, perfect after a day of exploring the city.

Top Restaurants for Fine Dining & Casual Eats

From **Michelin-starred restaurants** to **charming bistros**, Durham offers a diverse range of dining options that will suit every taste and occasion. Whether you're looking for a **romantic evening out** or a **casual bite with friends**, you'll find something to satisfy every craving.

The Cellar Door

For those seeking an exceptional **fine dining experience**, **The Cellar Door** is one of Durham's top-rated restaurants. Located just a short stroll from the cathedral, this intimate, **award-winning restaurant** serves up exquisite dishes made with **locally sourced ingredients**. The menu changes seasonally, but you can expect to find dishes like **pan-seared scallops with butternut squash** or **roast venison with blackberries**. The **elegant atmosphere**, paired with expertly paired wines, makes this the ideal spot for a **special evening**.

The Coach House

For a more casual yet equally delicious experience, **The Coach House** offers **modern British cuisine** in a relaxed setting. The dishes here are both inventive and comforting, featuring **local, seasonal ingredients** with a creative twist. You might find a dish like **pan-fried hake with a pea and mint purée**, or **roast chicken with lemon and thyme**, paired with **roast potatoes** that are crisp on the outside and soft on the inside. The **welcoming atmosphere** and **friendly service** make it a great spot for both families and couples.

Ramside Hall Hotel

Located just outside Durham, **Ramside Hall Hotel** is home to the **Ramside Restaurant**, a **Michelin-recommended** eatery that offers a more **elevated dining experience**. Whether you're indulging in **afternoon tea**, or dining on **tender lamb racks** or **steaks cooked to perfection**, this restaurant offers a full range of dishes with flair and sophistication. The restaurant's contemporary design and **luxurious setting** make it a place to dress up and enjoy an unforgettable meal.

Cozy Cafés & Afternoon Tea Spots

Durham's café culture is an invitation to **slow**

down, sip on a **perfectly brewed coffee**, and indulge in a **slice of cake**. These cozy spots are the ideal places to **escape the hustle and bustle** of the city and unwind for a bit.

Flat White Café

For coffee aficionados, the **Flat White Café** is a must-visit. Nestled in the heart of Durham, this charming café serves up rich, **smooth flat whites** made with **locally roasted beans**. The interior is **warm and inviting**, with exposed brick walls, cozy armchairs, and large windows where you can sit and people-watch as you sip your coffee. Don't miss their **homemade cakes**, including **carrot cake** and **chocolate brownies**, which perfectly complement your drink.

The Tea House

For the quintessential **afternoon tea experience**, head to **The Tea House**. This delightful café offers an assortment of freshly brewed teas paired with **scones, finger sandwiches**, and **fancy pastries**. The soft, **delicate flavors** of the teas blend beautifully with the rich, **buttery scones**, making this the perfect place to indulge in a traditional English pastime. Whether you're visiting with friends or enjoying some **alone time**, the charming atmosphere and **exceptional service** make this café a true gem.

Durham's Food Markets & Street Vendors – Where to Find Fresh & Local Produce

If you want to experience the **fresh flavors of Durham**, there's no better way than to visit one of its **food markets** or explore the **street vendors** that line the city's streets. These bustling hubs are where locals come to find the finest **local produce**, **artisanal goods**, and **tasty street food**.

Durham Indoor Market

For a truly local experience, head to the **Durham Indoor Market**, where you'll find an array of **fresh produce** including seasonal fruits, vegetables, and meats sourced from the surrounding countryside. The market is also home to **local food vendors**, selling everything from freshly made **pies** to **smoked fish** and **cheese**. It's the perfect spot to sample the freshest ingredients and bring a little taste of Durham home with you.

Durham Street Food

On weekends, Durham's **street food scene** comes alive, offering everything from **handmade pizza** to **gourmet burgers** and **Mexican street tacos**. Visit the **Food Festival** or the **open-air markets**, where you'll find delicious **local fare** and discover new flavors from around the world. These street vendors provide a fun and relaxed way to sample the **diverse tastes** of Durham, and there's always something to suit every craving.

Finally Durham's food and drink scene is a **celebration of local flavors**, from **traditional dishes** to contemporary dining experiences. Whether you're enjoying a hearty meal in a **historic pub** or sipping a **deliciously brewed ale** on a **sunny terrace**, Durham promises to delight your taste buds and leave you with unforgettable memories of its **culinary wonders**.

Family-Friendly Activities in Durham

Durham is not only a destination for history buffs and culture enthusiasts but also a fantastic spot for family fun! With a rich mix of outdoor adventures, interactive museums, and child-friendly activities, it's a place where families can create lasting memories while exploring together. Whether you're seeking a relaxing day in nature, hands-on learning experiences, or fun-filled adventures for all ages, Durham has something for everyone in the family to enjoy!

Durham's Best Parks & Playgrounds

Durham is home to some of the most picturesque and inviting parks, perfect for children to run around, explore, and have a blast! Let's explore the best places to enjoy outdoor fun that will keep both little ones and adults entertained.

Wharton Park

Wharton Park, located just a short walk from the city center, is the perfect spot to spend a day outdoors. This lovely park offers **spacious lawns** and **fantastic playgrounds** with equipment designed for various age groups. From **swings** and **slides** to climbing frames, there's plenty to keep your kids entertained. The park's **wide-open spaces** are perfect for a family picnic, while you enjoy the **spectacular views** of Durham Cathedral and the surrounding countryside. It's a wonderful place for families to relax, unwind, and enjoy the fresh air.

Durham Riverside Walk & Play Park

Another gem is the **Durham Riverside Walk & Play Park**, where you can stroll along the banks of the River Wear and let the kids play at the **adventure playground**. This scenic park is not only an ideal spot for a family walk but also has a **sandpit, climbing walls**, and **slides**, providing the perfect mix of adventure and outdoor play. The Riverside Walk itself is stroller-friendly, so even the youngest family members can enjoy the beauty of the river while the older ones let off some steam in the playground.

The DLI Museum and Durham Art Gallery Gardens

The DLI Museum may have fascinating history exhibits, but the **gardens outside** are perfect for children to explore and enjoy. With **wide lawns** to run on and **beautiful flower beds**, the kids can enjoy the outdoors while you relax and take in the views. It's a lovely setting for families to enjoy together!

Family-Friendly Attractions & Museums – Interactive Learning Experiences

Durham is a treasure trove of **interactive museums** and **fun attractions** that will inspire your child's imagination and curiosity. These educational spots are designed to engage the whole family with hands-on exhibits and activities.

The Durham Museum & Heritage Centre

Step back in time at the **Durham Museum & Heritage Centre**, where kids can learn about the city's rich history in a fun and interactive way. The museum offers **hands-on exhibits** and **interactive displays** that are perfect for young minds. Children will love exploring the **Roman artifacts**, **Victorian exhibitions**, and discovering the history behind Durham's famous cathedral. The museum also often hosts **workshops** and **family-friendly events**, making it an exciting destination for kids to dive into Durham's fascinating past.

The Oriental Museum

For families interested in world cultures, the **Oriental Museum** is a must-see. It's one of the UK's leading museums of **Eastern art and culture**, and it's packed with **interactive displays** that will captivate both kids and adults. With everything from **ancient Egyptian treasures** to **Chinese ceramics**, there's so much to explore. The museum often offers **family activities** like **craft sessions** or **cultural workshops**, allowing children to get involved with the exhibits and create something to take home.

The Botanic Garden

Looking for a place where your kids can connect with nature? Head over to the **Durham University Botanic Garden**, where the whole family can enjoy exploring the **winding paths**, **greenhouses**, and **beautiful plants** from around the world. The **children's garden** is designed especially for young explorers, offering hands-on gardening activities and the chance to learn about different plants and wildlife in a fun and educational way. Be sure to check out their family workshops, which are perfect for little green thumbs!

Child-Friendly Walking & Cycling Routes – Easy & Safe Trails for All Ages

Exploring Durham's natural beauty on foot or by bike is a fantastic way to spend quality time as a family. With safe and scenic routes for all abilities, it's the perfect way to keep the kids active while enjoying the sights of Durham's countryside.

Durham Riverside Walk

The **Durham Riverside Walk** is a **stroller-friendly trail** that offers a peaceful, scenic route along the River Wear. Starting from **Wharton Park**, you can stroll through beautiful green spaces, pass the **Durham Cathedral**, and enjoy the views of the river. It's a relaxed, easy route that children of all ages will love, and there are plenty of opportunities to stop along the way for a family picnic. You can also bring bikes if your little ones are into cycling—this flat, easy-going path is perfect for young riders.

Croxdale Park to Aykley Heads

This **family-friendly walking route** takes you through the lush **Croxdale Park** and into **Aykley Heads**, where you'll find scenic countryside views and charming landscapes. The route is gentle and **child-friendly**, making it ideal for younger kids, and it's a great way to introduce them to the joys of nature. Keep an eye out for local wildlife—there's always something new to discover along the way!

The Derwent Walk

If you're looking for a cycling route that's a bit more adventurous, check out the **Derwent Walk**. This **family-friendly cycling route** is well-maintained and takes you through some of the most beautiful parts of County Durham. With its easy-to-navigate paths and pretty landscapes, it's perfect for a fun-filled day of family cycling. The route is safe, making it an excellent option for younger cyclists who want to explore Durham on two wheels.

Hands-on Learning Experiences & Workshops – Educational & Fun Activities

There's no better way for kids to learn than by getting their hands dirty and getting involved! Durham offers plenty of opportunities for kids to try out new skills, craft something cool, and enjoy a **hands-on learning experience**.

The Clayworks

At **The Clayworks**, kids can unleash their creativity with fun and **hands-on pottery workshops**. Whether they're shaping a little clay animal or creating their own masterpieces, this is the place for budding artists to get their hands dirty and make something special. The Clayworks offers a relaxed atmosphere where kids can learn the art of pottery while having fun, and parents can join in too! It's a great way for the whole family to try their hand at something new.

The Dairy Barn

For a more farm-inspired adventure, take the kids to **The Dairy Barn** where they can learn all about farm life. This **interactive farm experience** allows children to feed animals, learn about the **dairy industry**, and even try their hand at **making butter** or **cheese**. It's the perfect way for kids to get their hands involved in something educational and fun, all while learning where their food comes from!

Durham Markets – Crafts & Local Workshops

Durham's local markets are more than just places to buy fresh produce—they're also great spots for family-friendly **craft workshops** and **art sessions**. You'll often find **local artisans** offering activities like **painting**, **woodwork**, or **jewelry making**, perfect for kids to try their hand at something creative. The markets are full of vibrant energy, and your kids will love the chance to make their own souvenirs while exploring the wonderful local products on offer.

Durham is truly a place where families can make the most of every moment. From **interactive museums** to **hands-on workshops** and **outdoor adventures**, there are endless opportunities for fun and learning. Whether you're spending a relaxed day at the park or embarking on a cycling adventure, you'll find that Durham is a wonderful place for creating family memories that will last a lifetime. So pack up the little ones, put on your adventure hats, and get ready to explore all the amazing family-friendly activities Durham has to offer!

Outdoor Adventures & Nature Escapes in Durham

Durham is a haven for nature lovers, outdoor enthusiasts, and those who crave adventure. From the rolling hills of its countryside to the dramatic coastline, the region offers a wealth of opportunities to explore, breathe in the fresh air, and immerse yourself in its natural beauty. Whether you're lacing up your hiking boots, grabbing your binoculars for some wildlife watching, or looking to enjoy water-based activities, Durham will satisfy your craving for outdoor adventure.

Walking Trails & Hiking Routes

The diverse landscape of Durham offers a range of hiking and walking routes, making it a **paradise** for those who love to explore on foot. From **easy city strolls** to more challenging **country hikes**, there's something for every kind of adventurer.

Durham City Riverside Walk

Start your adventure with a **leisurely city walk** along the banks of the **River Wear**. This scenic route winds through lush greenery, offering some of the best views of **Durham Cathedral** and the **city skyline**. Whether you're a seasoned walker or just looking for a relaxing stroll, this walk is perfect. The well-maintained path takes you along the river, through parks, and past quaint historic sites, making it a delightful route for a **half-day adventure**. It's a great way to start exploring Durham's picturesque beauty while being right in the heart of the city.

The Weardale Way

For a more rural escape, head out to the **Weardale Way**, a **long-distance walking trail** that stretches across the stunning **Durham Dales**. This 80-mile trail will lead you through picturesque **villages**, vast **moorlands**, and lush **valleys**, offering breathtaking views at every turn. The route is well-marked and passes through areas of natural beauty, making it a **must-do** for nature enthusiasts and keen hikers. Whether you're hiking for the day or taking it on as a multi-day adventure, the Weardale Way immerses you in the charm of rural Durham.

Hamsterley Forest

For those looking for an adventurous woodland experience, **Hamsterley Forest** offers a network of **trails** and **woodland paths** perfect for hiking, biking, and just exploring nature. With miles of trails winding through ancient oak trees, fern-filled valleys, and bubbling streams, this is a place where you can truly connect with the forest. Whether you want a **gentle ramble** or a more challenging hike, **Hamsterley Forest** provides a peaceful and rejuvenating escape from city life. The forest is also home to a variety of wildlife, so keep your eyes peeled for deer, red squirrels, and a range of bird species.

Wildlife Watching & Nature Reserves – Best Spots for Birdwatching & Nature Lovers

Durham is a fantastic destination for wildlife watchers and nature lovers, offering an abundance of **nature reserves**, **birdwatching spots**, and diverse ecosystems to explore. Whether you're keen to spot elusive species or simply want to enjoy the tranquillity of nature, Durham has plenty of places to immerse yourself in its wild side.

Durham Nature Reserves

Durham boasts several **protected nature reserves**, perfect for nature lovers. **Low Barns Nature Reserve**, for instance, is a peaceful haven for birdwatchers. Situated on the **River Wear**, it's home to a range of **wetland birds** and offers delightful walking paths where you can explore the **reed beds**, **wildflower meadows**, and peaceful ponds. It's an ideal spot for **birdwatching**—you might see anything from **kingfishers** and **swans** to **wildfowl** and **waders**. The reserve also features an **educational visitor center**, making it both a peaceful retreat and a chance to learn more about the local ecosystem.

The North Pennines Area of Outstanding Natural Beauty (AONB)

For more rugged, highland wildlife watching, visit the **North Pennines AONB**, an area rich in wildlife and stunning landscapes. This region is home to unique species such as the **red grouse**, **golden plover**, and the elusive **barn owl**. The **moorlands** and **heather-clad hills** are the ideal habitat for these creatures, and you can enjoy watching them in their natural environment. Additionally, the **Raby Castle Estate** offers guided wildlife tours, where you'll get the chance to spot **red deer** and **wild boar**, as well as enjoy an educational experience about the wildlife conservation efforts in the region.

Teesdale Wildlife

The beautiful valley of **Teesdale** is another spot brimming with wildlife. As you wander along the **River Tees**, keep your eyes open for a variety of species, including the majestic **kingfisher**, **otters**, and **grey herons**. The valley is a haven for **birdwatching**, with **woodpeckers**, **swallows**, and even **peregrine falcons** often spotted in the area. Whether you're walking along the riverbanks or through the valleys, Teesdale offers a **serene** and **beautiful natural setting** for nature enthusiasts.

Fishing & Water Sports in Durham – Where to Enjoy Angling & Boating

For those who love spending time on the water, Durham offers a variety of **fishing spots** and **water sports activities** that allow you to immerse yourself in nature while enjoying a day on the water. Whether you're into **angling**, **canoeing**, or **boating**, Durham's waterways provide the perfect backdrop for water-based fun.

Angling at the River Wear

For keen anglers, the **River Wear** offers some of the best fishing opportunities in the region. Known for its **salmon**, **trout**, and **grayling**, the river is a popular spot for fishing enthusiasts. Whether you're an experienced fisherman or a beginner, the calm, meandering waters provide ample chances to cast your line and relax. The **riverbanks** are lined with lush vegetation, and the tranquil surroundings offer a peaceful environment to spend the day. You can also enjoy the added bonus of stunning views of **Durham Cathedral** while you fish!

Boating on the River Wear

For a more adventurous water experience, why not try **boating on the River Wear**? Whether you're kayaking, canoeing, or paddleboarding, the river offers a fantastic way to get closer to nature. Paddling down the river lets you enjoy **close-up views** of Durham's **landmarks** from a whole new perspective. You can also take a **boat tour** for a more relaxed experience and learn about Durham's

history, while soaking in the natural beauty of the surrounding landscape.

Fishing at Grassholme Reservoir

For a more serene fishing experience, **Grassholme Reservoir** is a great spot to cast your line and unwind. Known for its still waters and beautiful backdrop of hills, this reservoir is ideal for **fly fishing**. You can enjoy a **peaceful day** by the water, surrounded by nature, while trying to catch some of the large **rainbow trout** that inhabit the reservoir. It's a relaxing escape for anglers looking to enjoy Durham's natural beauty.

The Durham Heritage Coast – A Scenic and Historic Coastal Experience

Durham is also home to a striking stretch of coastline—the **Durham Heritage Coast**—that offers not only **breathtaking views** but also a fascinating glimpse into the region's maritime past. This section of the **North East coastline** stretches for around **11 miles**, from **Horden** to **South Shields**, and is a place of stunning cliffs, sandy beaches, and rich history.

Exploring the Coastline

Take a walk along the **Durham Heritage Coastline**, and you'll be treated to dramatic **sea cliffs**, **hidden coves**, and panoramic views of the North Sea. The **cliffs** are home to an array of **wildlife**, including **seabirds** like **kittiwakes** and **razorbills**, making it a great spot for birdwatching. The coastal path offers various walking routes, so you can take it slow and enjoy the views, or tackle a more challenging hike for a sense of accomplishment.

History at Blackhall Rocks

Visit **Blackhall Rocks**, where you can explore the rich industrial and mining history of the region. The **cliffs** here have stories to tell, and as you walk along the shoreline, you'll be able to spot the remnants of **old mining villages**, **abandoned pits**, and **ancient shipwrecks**. The rugged beauty of the coastline combined with its rich history makes it a fascinating place to explore and one of the most rewarding nature escapes in Durham.

Durham's natural beauty is as diverse as it is exhilarating, offering everything from tranquil waters and ancient forests to rugged cliffs and scenic coastlines. Whether you're hiking through peaceful valleys, fishing on quiet rivers, or simply soaking in the view from a coastal path, Durham offers endless outdoor adventures for nature lovers and thrill-seekers alike. Get out there and start exploring—Durham's wild beauty is waiting!

Shopping & Markets in Durham

Durham is a city where history meets modern charm, and nowhere is this blend more evident than in its shopping scene. Whether you're wandering through the **bustling indoor markets**, browsing **high-end boutiques**, or discovering **hidden treasures in antique stores**, Durham offers a rich and varied shopping experience. From **handmade crafts** to **local delicacies**, every corner of the city invites you to explore, uncover hidden gems, and take home a piece of Durham's unique character.

If you love the thrill of discovering **one-of-a-kind souvenirs**, the joy of shopping for **locally made goods**, or the satisfaction of finding **a rare antique**, Durham will keep you intrigued at every turn. So grab your shopping bag and get ready for an adventure through **Durham's markets, shops, and artisanal boutiques**!

Durham Indoor Market – Handmade Goods, Fresh Produce & Local Crafts

Hidden in the heart of Durham's city centre is the **Durham Indoor Market**, a **vibrant marketplace** packed with over **50 independent traders** offering everything from **fresh produce** to **handcrafted goods**. Stepping inside feels like entering a treasure trove of **local culture and tradition**—the air is filled with the **aroma of fresh bread**, the **chatter of friendly stallholders**, and the **vivid colors of handmade crafts and clothing**.

A Foodie's Delight

For food lovers, the market is a paradise. **Artisan cheeses, organic meats, and homemade jams** line the stalls, tempting you with their **freshness and local charm**. You'll find **farm-fresh vegetables, locally sourced honey**, and **traditional pies** that capture the essence of Durham's countryside. If you're looking for an authentic taste of the region, grab a **stottie cake** (a soft, thick bread roll) or a **chunky slice of locally made fudge**.

Handmade & Unique Treasures

Beyond food, Durham Indoor Market is a haven for **craft lovers**. Stalls offer

hand-knitted scarves, artisan jewelry, and **locally produced pottery**—perfect gifts for those who appreciate the beauty of handmade goods. Vintage lovers will find **second-hand books, retro clothing,** and **quirky home décor,** making it easy to leave with something truly special.

Whether you're on the hunt for **fresh food, handcrafted gifts, or a taste of local culture,** Durham Indoor Market is an **unmissable shopping destination** that brings the city's history and creativity to life.

High Street Shopping & Boutique Store

Durham's **high street** is a **vibrant blend** of **big-name brands, charming boutiques, and independent retailers,** making it a **shopper's paradise.** Whether you're after **fashion, books, home décor, or artisan chocolates,** Durham's high street offers something for every taste.

Independent Boutiques & Unique Finds

For those who prefer **boutique shopping,** Durham is full of **hidden gems.** Explore charming streets like **Elvet Bridge** and **Silver**

Street, where you'll find **independent fashion stores**, **handmade crafts**, and **locally owned bookshops**. These quaint stores offer everything from **vintage-inspired clothing** to **hand-stitched leather bags**, making it easy to take home something **truly one-of-a-kind**.

Designer & High-Street Fashion

For a mix of **designer labels and high-street staples**, **Prince Bishops Shopping Centre** and **The Riverwalk** offer a great selection of clothing, accessories, and beauty products. Whether you're hunting for a **stylish new outfit**, **luxury skincare**, or **the latest trends**, Durham's shopping scene is sure to satisfy.

From **quirky independent stores** to **well-loved fashion brands**, Durham's high street is full of **exciting discoveries** for shoppers who love variety.

Antique Shops & Art Galleries

If you love the thrill of **hunting for hidden treasures**, Durham's **antique shops and art galleries** will not disappoint. Tucked away in **narrow lanes and historic buildings**, these spots are perfect for collectors, art lovers, and anyone looking for something **truly unique**.

Antique Stores – A Journey Through Time

Durham is home to a number of **antique and vintage shops**, offering everything from **rare books** to **Victorian-era furniture**. Shops like **Durham Antiques & Interiors** and **The Curious Curio** are filled with **old maps, vintage jewellery, and historical trinkets**, allowing you to take home a **piece of Durham's past**. Whether you're after **delicate porcelain**, **weathered leather-bound novels**, or **one-of-a-kind home décor**, there's always something fascinating to uncover.

Art Galleries – A Celebration of Creativity

For art enthusiasts, Durham has **several exceptional galleries** showcasing both **local talent and internationally recognized artists**. The **Gala Gallery** and **The Art Shop & Gallery** feature an eclectic mix of **paintings, sculptures, and ceramics**, highlighting the work of **Northeast artists**.

Many pieces capture Durham's **historic beauty**, making them a perfect souvenir for those who want a lasting memory of the city.

For those looking to decorate their home with **one-of-a-kind artwork** or find a **thoughtful gift**, Durham's antique shops and galleries offer a **rich and rewarding shopping experience**.

Best Places to Buy Durham Souvenirs

No trip to Durham is complete without taking home a **special souvenir**. Whether you want to remember **the city's history, its flavors**, or **its craftsmanship**, there are plenty of great options to choose from.

Locally Made Food & Drinks

Durham is famous for **artisan food products**, and these make for **delicious souvenirs**. Some of the best **edible gifts** include:

- **Durham Gin** – A locally distilled gin infused with unique botanicals.

- **Handmade fudge** – Found in sweet shops and markets, these make for a delightful treat.
- **Stottie cakes** – A traditional North East bread, great for those who love to cook at home.

Traditional Durham Crafts

For those who prefer **handmade keepsakes**, Durham's **artisan shops and markets** offer plenty of beautiful items:

- **Locally made pottery** – Inspired by Durham's landscapes and traditions.
- **Handwoven textiles** – Wool scarves and blankets made in traditional mills.
- **Durham Cathedral souvenirs** – Beautiful prints, mugs, and books about the city's most famous landmark.

Books & Historical Memorabilia

Durham has a **rich literary history**, and you'll find **plenty of bookshops** offering **historical texts, novels set in Durham, and antique prints**. These make for **thoughtful souvenirs**, perfect for anyone who loves **history and storytelling**.

Where to Find the Best Souvenirs?

- **Durham Cathedral Shop** – For historical books and cathedral-themed gifts.
- **The People's Bookshop** – An independent bookshop offering rare and second-hand books.
- **Durham Indoor Market** – A great place to find local crafts, food, and unique gifts.

From **delicious food** to **handmade crafts**, Durham's souvenirs capture the **heart and soul of the city**, making them **perfect mementos** of your visit.

Final Thoughts: Shopping in Durham

Shopping in Durham is more than just a pastime—it's an **adventure!** Whether you're exploring the **historic indoor market**, **browsing boutique stores**, or **hunting for antiques**, every corner of the city offers **something special**. Durham's shopping scene is a **perfect mix of tradition and modernity**, ensuring that **no matter what you're looking for, you'll find something**

that captures the essence of this incredible city.

So go ahead—**explore, discover, and take a little piece of Durham home with you!**

Seasonal Events & Festivals in Durham (2025)

There's something truly magical about Durham throughout the year. No matter the season, the city comes alive with vibrant celebrations that bring together history, culture, and community spirit. From **grand processions honoring its mining heritage** to **dazzling winter lights**, **food festivals that ignite the senses**, and **student celebrations that fill the streets with energy**, Durham's calendar is packed with events that are as exciting as they are unforgettable.

I've been lucky enough to experience Durham in all its seasonal splendor, and let me tell you—there's no place quite like it. Whether you're a **history buff**, a **lover of festive cheer**, a **foodie in search of new flavors**, or simply someone who enjoys **a great celebration**, this city knows how to throw an event! So, let's dive into Durham's **must-experience festivals of 2025**—because trust me, you don't want to miss them.

Durham Miners' Gala – A Historic Gathering of the Mining Community

If you want to witness **Durham's heart and soul** in full force, there's no better event than the **Durham Miners' Gala**. Held every **July**, this is more than just a festival—it's a **proud and powerful tradition**. Walking through the city on Gala Day, you can feel the **energy and emotion** in the air.

I still remember the first time I saw the **colossal banners** waving above the crowds, each one representing a different mining lodge, each one telling a story of the past. The **brass bands** play their stirring music, their sound echoing through the historic streets, while thousands march in a **procession of solidarity**. This is a festival that honors the **strength, sacrifice, and community spirit** of Durham's mining families.

By mid-morning, **the streets are packed**, and the procession winds its way towards **Durham Cathedral**, where a moving memorial service takes place. Then, the city turns into one big, buzzing **celebration**, with speeches, live music, and plenty of **pubs overflowing with laughter and** conversation. It's an **incredibly moving and uplifting experience**, one that connects the past with the present in a way that only Durham can.

If you're visiting in July, make sure you **join the crowds**, grab a pint, and soak in **one of the most historic gatherings in the UK.**

Lumiere Durham Festival – A Stunning Citywide Light Display

Now, let's talk about **pure magic**. Imagine Durham's **ancient streets and landmarks** transformed into a breathtaking **kaleidoscope of light, color, and creativity**. That's **Lumiere Durham**, the UK's largest **light festival**, and it's unlike anything you've ever seen.

Held every **two years in November**, Lumiere turns the city into a **spectacular open-air gallery**, where buildings, bridges, and even the riverbanks become **canvas for dazzling installations**. Walking through the festival feels like stepping into a **dreamlike world**, where **cathedrals glow, streets shimmer**, and **unexpected corners become sources of wonder.**

One of my favorite memories was seeing **Durham Cathedral** bathed in mesmerizing patterns of light, as if it had been **painted with the stars themselves**. Then there were **the floating lanterns along the River Wear**, gently swaying as if telling whispered stories of the city's past.

Lumiere is **free to attend**, and whether you visit for an evening stroll or dedicate an entire night to exploring its wonders, **it's an experience that stays with you long after the lights fade**.

Durham Christmas Festival & Markets

Ah, Durham at **Christmas**—it's like stepping straight into a **winter wonderland**. The city, already beautiful, becomes even more enchanting as **twinkling lights**, **festive music**, and the **scent of mulled wine** fill the air.

The **Durham Christmas Festival** is a **three-day extravaganza** that transforms the city into a **haven of festive cheer**. The main attraction? The **huge marquee market** in the shadow of **Durham Cathedral**, where local artisans and vendors sell everything from handmade crafts and gifts to **seasonal delicacies**.

I can never resist **a warm mince pie** and a **steaming cup of spiced cider** while wandering through the market. The streets are alive with **carol singers**, and if you listen closely, you might even hear the **echo of sleigh bells** as horse-drawn carriages make their way through the cobbled lanes.

For families, there's **a magical Santa's grotto**, and for thrill-seekers, the **open-air ice rink** at **The Riverwalk** offers a chance to skate beneath the festive lights. There's something about Christmas in Durham that feels **intimate and timeless**, like the city itself is wrapped in a warm holiday hug.

Spring & Summer Food Festivals – Celebrating Local & International Cuisine

Now, if you're a **food lover**, you need to mark Durham's **Spring and Summer Food Festivals** on your calendar. These are the kind of events that **wake up your taste buds** and **introduce you to flavors you'll never forget**.

In **May**, the **Bishop Auckland Food Festival** (just a short drive from Durham) brings together **top chefs, street food vendors, and artisan producers** for a weekend of **indulgence and discovery**. Imagine tasting **locally made cheeses**, sipping on **Durham-distilled gin**, and watching **live cooking demos** from celebrity chefs.

Come **July**, it's time for the **Durham Summer Food Festival**, where the riverside comes alive with **barbecue stalls, craft beer tents, and pop-up restaurants** offering flavors from around the world.

Whether you're craving **classic fish and chips**, **Indian street food**, or **gourmet pastries**, Durham's food festivals are a **feast for the senses**. Bring your appetite—because trust me, you'll want to try **everything**!

Durham University Events & Open Days

Durham isn't just a city of history—it's a **hub of learning and innovation**, and that energy comes alive during the university's **many events and open days**.

In **March and June**, Durham University throws open its doors for **prospective students and curious visitors** to explore its **historic colleges, world-class research centers, and stunning libraries**.

I remember walking through **Castle College**, feeling the weight of history in its stone walls, and standing in **Palace Green Library**, imagining the countless minds that had studied there before me. Even if you're not planning to enroll, the **public lectures, exhibitions, and performances** held throughout the year offer **a fascinating glimpse into the university's vibrant academic life**.

For sports fans, the **Durham Regatta in June** is a must-see, as **rowing teams race along the River Wear**, filling the city with **cheers and excitement**.

Final Thoughts: Durham's Year-Round Festivities Await You!

No matter when you visit Durham, there's always **something to celebrate**. From **deep-rooted traditions** to **dazzling modern festivals,** this city knows how to bring people together.

I've felt the **pride and power** of the Miners' Gala, been **enchanted by Lumiere's lights**, and **warmed by the festive glow of Christmas markets**. I've tasted flavors that linger on my tongue long after the festival ends, and I've soaked in the **university's energy and excitement**.

So, if you're looking for a place where **history, culture, and celebration** collide in the most spectacular way—**Durham is waiting for you**.

Practical Travel Tips & Resources for Visiting Durham

Visiting Durham is an exciting adventure, whether you're coming for the **history, stunning landscapes, delicious food, or vibrant festivals**. But like any trip, a little preparation goes a long way. Over the years, I've learned that knowing a few **local customs, safety tips, budget hacks, and emergency contacts** can make all the difference between a smooth, stress-free visit and unexpected hiccups.

So, if you're planning your Durham trip, **let me help you feel confident and prepared**. I'll walk you through everything you need to know, from how to **greet locals properly** to **how to save a few pounds** while still enjoying the best experiences Durham has to offer. Let's dive in!

Local Customs & Etiquette – What Visitors Should Know

One of my favorite things about Durham is **how friendly and welcoming the people are**. Whether you're chatting with a **local**

shop owner, **ordering a pint at the pub**, or **asking for directions**, you'll find that most people are happy to help. That said, here are a few things to keep in mind to ensure you make the best impression:

Greetings & Politeness

- **A simple "hello" or "hi" works just fine** when greeting someone. If you're feeling extra polite, you can say "good morning" or "good afternoon."
- **People in Durham appreciate manners.** Saying **"please" and "thank you"** goes a long way.
- If someone helps you, a friendly **"cheers" (British slang for thanks)** is always appreciated.

Pub & Dining Etiquette

- In **traditional British pubs**, it's customary to **order your drinks at the bar** rather than wait for table service.
- If you're in a group, locals often **take turns buying rounds of drinks**—so if someone buys you a pint, it's expected that you'll get the next round.

- Tipping in restaurants isn't as rigid as in some other countries, but **leaving 10-12% for good service is common**.

Queueing (Lining Up) is a Big Deal

- Whether you're waiting for a **bus, ATM, or takeaway, always respect the queue**. Brits take queuing seriously, and **cutting in line is a major no-no!**

Safety Tips for Tourists – Staying Secure in Durham

Durham is generally **a very safe city**, and I've always felt comfortable walking around—even at night. But, like anywhere, it's good to **stay aware and take basic precautions**. Here are a few key safety tips:

General Safety

- **The city center is well-lit and patrolled**—but if you're out late, **stick to well-populated areas**.
- **Be mindful in crowded places** like markets, festivals, or busy

pubs—**pickpocketing is rare, but not unheard of**.

Public Transport & Taxis

- If using a taxi, **only book through licensed taxi firms** or use a **registered ride-hailing app** like Uber.
- Durham's buses are generally safe, but it's always best to **keep your belongings close** when traveling.

Weather & Walking Safety

- If you're exploring **Durham's scenic countryside**, be prepared! **Weather can change quickly**, so bring **a waterproof jacket and sturdy walking shoes**.
- **Watch out for slippery cobblestones** in the historic center, especially in winter.

Emergency Contacts

- **Police, Fire, Ambulance:** Dial **999** for emergencies
- **Non-Emergency Police Help:** Dial **101**

- **Local Taxi Services:** Keep a couple of local taxi numbers saved in case you need a ride back.

Budget Travel Tips & Money-Saving Hacks

Durham is **packed with amazing experiences**, and the best part? **You don't need to spend a fortune to enjoy them!** Here are some budget-friendly ways to explore the city:

Affordable Accommodation

- Stay in **guest houses or B&Bs** instead of hotels—many offer **charming stays at a lower price**.
- Durham University rents out **student accommodation during the summer**, which is a **cheap and convenient option** for travelers.
- **Durham Cathedral is free to enter**, though donations are encouraged.
- **Take advantage of the city's many free walking trails**—including the beautiful **Riverside Walk**.
- Many museums, like the **Durham Museum and Heritage Centre**, offer **low-cost entry fees**.

Eating & Drinking on a Budget

- **Look for meal deals in local pubs**—many offer **discounted lunch menus** during the week.
- Visit **Durham's food markets for affordable local produce and street food**.
- If you love coffee and pastries, some **cafés offer discounts if you bring your own reusable cup**.

Useful Contacts & Emergency Information

I always like to **save key phone numbers and addresses on my phone before I travel**, just in case. Here are the most useful contacts for Durham:

Emergency Services

- **Police, Fire, Ambulance:** Dial **999** for emergencies
- **Non-Emergency Police Help:** Dial **101**

Hospitals & Medical Help

- **University Hospital of North Durham:** +44 191 333 2333
- **NHS 111 Service:** Call **111** for medical advice if it's not an emergency.

Tourist Information

- **Durham Visitor Information Centre**: Market Place, Durham, DH1 3NJ
- **Phone:** +44 300 026 6985

Local Transport

- **Durham Bus Information:** +44 191 420 5050
- **Train Station Enquiries:** National Rail - **03457 48 49 50**

Sustainable & Responsible Tourism in Durham

If you love to travel, chances are you also **want to protect the beautiful places you visit**. Durham is rich in **natural beauty and heritage**, so traveling responsibly helps preserve it for future generations. Here are some **easy ways to be a more sustainable traveler** in Durham:

Use Public Transport & Walk When Possible

- Durham is a **compact city**, and you can **easily explore on foot**.
- If you need to travel further, use **buses, trains, or bicycles** instead of driving.

Support Local Businesses

- **Shop at independent stores and markets** instead of big chains.
- Eat at **locally owned restaurants** that use **seasonal, regional ingredients**.

Reduce Plastic Waste

- Carry a **reusable water bottle**—Durham has plenty of **public water fountains**.
- Say **no to plastic bags** and use a **reusable shopping bag** when exploring the markets.

Respect Nature & Wildlife

- If you're hiking or visiting the Durham Heritage Coast, always **follow marked trails** and **take your rubbish with you**.

- Keep a respectful distance from **wildlife and natural habitats**.

Final Thoughts: You're Ready for Durham!

I hope these **practical tips** help you feel **more prepared and confident** for your visit to Durham. Whether it's **understanding local customs, staying safe, finding budget-friendly options**, or **traveling sustainably**, a little planning goes a long way.

Durham is a city that **welcomes visitors with open arms**, and I can't wait for you to experience **its rich history, stunning landscapes, and warm community spirit. Pack your bags, get ready for adventure, and most of all—enjoy every moment!**

Suggested Itineraries for Every Traveler in Durham

Welcome to Durham! Whether you're here for just a day, a weekend, or a longer adventure, I've got you covered. There's something about this city that makes every visit feel special—maybe it's the **medieval charm**, the **stunning natural landscapes**, or just the **warm and friendly atmosphere**.

I've spent plenty of time wandering Durham's cobbled streets, uncovering **hidden corners, local favorites, and must-see attractions**. So, let me help you **craft the perfect itinerary**—whether you're a history buff, an outdoor enthusiast, a family traveler, or someone who just loves stumbling upon the unexpected.

One-Day Itinerary: Key Highlights & Quick Tours

If you only have **one day in Durham**, don't worry—you can still experience the city's magic. This itinerary is all about **hitting the highlights without feeling rushed**.

Morning: A Historic Start

- **Durham Cathedral** – Start your day with **one of the most breathtaking sights in England**. The towering Gothic architecture, the intricate stained glass, and the **tranquil cloisters** (yes, Harry Potter fans, this is where Hogwarts scenes were filmed!) make this a must-visit.
- **Durham Castle** – Right next door, this Norman fortress is a fascinating glimpse into the city's medieval past. If you can, **join a guided tour** to hear its incredible stories.

Afternoon: Riverside Stroll & Local Eats

- **Walk along the River Wear** – The loop around the **Riverside Walk** is peaceful and scenic, offering **stunning views of the cathedral**.
- **Lunch at Flat White Kitchen** – A local favorite for **amazing coffee and delicious brunch** (try the pancakes!).

Evening: Markets & Hidden Gems

- **Durham Indoor Market** – Explore this Victorian market hall full of **handmade crafts, fresh produce, and quirky gifts**.

- **A pint at Ye Old Elm Tree** – End the day with a drink at one of Durham's **coziest and most historic pubs**.

One day might not be enough, but it's a start—and you'll definitely want to return!

Weekend Itinerary: 2-Day Plans for a Short Escape

Got a **weekend in Durham**? Perfect. This itinerary gives you the best mix of **history, food, and outdoor adventure**.

Day 1: Exploring the Heart of Durham

- **Morning:** Start with **Durham Cathedral & Castle** (they're unmissable!).
- **Midday:** Take a leisurely **boat ride on the River Wear**—it's a fun and relaxing way to see the city from a different angle.
- **Afternoon:** Wander through **Durham's charming streets**, popping into independent shops and cafés.
- **Evening:** Have dinner at **Finbarr's**, a fantastic spot for **modern British cuisine**.

Day 2: Countryside & Culture

- **Morning:** Head out to **Beamish Museum**, a living history museum that **transports you back in time**.
- **Afternoon:** Visit **Crook Hall & Gardens**, a hidden gem where you can **enjoy traditional afternoon tea in a beautiful historic setting**.
- **Evening:** End the trip with **a relaxed meal at The Cellar Door**, a cozy restaurant overlooking the river.

Family-Friendly Itinerary: Activities for All Ages

If you're traveling with kids, Durham is **fantastic for families**. It's **walkable, full of fun attractions, and packed with adventures** for all ages.

Day 1: Playful & Educational

- **Morning:** Kick things off at **Durham University's Oriental Museum**—it's interactive, engaging, and filled with **fascinating treasures from around the world**.
- **Afternoon:** Let the kids burn off energy at **Wharton Park**, which has

playgrounds, picnic areas, and great views over the city**.
- **Evening:** Enjoy a **casual dinner at Tango**, a family-friendly spot known for its **delicious burgers**.

Day 2: Outdoor Fun

- **Morning:** Take a nature walk at **Hamsterley Forest**, where kids can **explore trails, go cycling, or even try a Gruffalo-themed walk**.
- **Afternoon:** Head to **Adventure Valley**, a fantastic outdoor play area with **farm animals, climbing zones, and go-karts**.
- **Evening:** End with a cozy meal at **The Library**, a relaxed restaurant with **great pizza options for kids**.

Historical & Cultural Itinerary

For history lovers, Durham is **an absolute treasure trove**. Here's how to **immerse yourself in its rich past**.

Day 1: Medieval Marvels

- **Morning:** Begin at **Durham Cathedral & Castle**—the city's most famous landmarks.
- **Afternoon:** Visit **Palace Green Library**, where you can see **rare manuscripts and historic exhibits**.
- **Evening:** Dine at **The Cellar Door**, housed in a historic building with medieval charm.

Day 2: Hidden History

- **Morning:** Explore **Beamish Museum**, an open-air museum where you can **step into the past**.
- **Afternoon:** Visit **Finchale Priory**, the **ruins of a medieval monastery** surrounded by peaceful countryside.
- **Evening:** Enjoy a drink at **The Shakespeare**, a pub with a history dating back centuries.

Nature & Adventure Itinerary

If you love **hiking, wildlife, and fresh air**, Durham has **plenty of outdoor adventures waiting for you**.

Day 1: Forest & Trails

- **Morning:** Start with a hike at **Durham Heritage Coast**—the dramatic cliffs and **seaside views are incredible**.
- **Afternoon:** Explore **Hamsterley Forest**, where you can **mountain bike, go horseback riding, or simply walk among the trees**.
- **Evening:** Unwind with a meal at **The Rose & Crown**, a countryside inn with **fantastic local dishes**.

Day 2: Water & Wildlife

- **Morning:** Try **paddleboarding or kayaking on the River Wear**—it's a peaceful and unique way to see Durham.
- **Afternoon:** Head to **Low Barns Nature Reserve**, a quiet spot for **birdwatching and walking trails**.
- **Evening:** Celebrate your adventure with a **hearty pub meal at The Kingslodge Inn**.

Off-the-Beaten-Path Itinerary: Hidden Gems & Local Secrets

For those who **love discovering lesser-known places**, this itinerary is packed with Durham's best-kept secrets.

Day 1: Secret Durham

- **Morning:** Visit **Old Durham Gardens,** a peaceful, historic spot that many visitors miss.
- **Afternoon:** Explore **Brancepeth Castle,** a privately owned castle with **occasional tours and events**.
- **Evening:** Grab dinner at **The Rabbit Hole,** a quirky **speakeasy-style restaurant** with live jazz.

Day 2: Unexpected Adventures

- **Morning:** Take a day trip to **Raby Castle,** one of the **most impressive historic estates in England**.
- **Afternoon:** Visit the **Botanic Garden,** a **serene escape with exotic plants and woodland trails**.
- **Evening:** End your adventure with a drink at **The Dun Cow,** a historic pub loved by locals.

Final Thoughts: Durham, Your Way

No matter your travel style, Durham **has something for everyone**. Whether you're here for **history, adventure, family fun, or**

hidden gems, this city welcomes you with **open arms and unforgettable experiences**.

Now, it's time to **pick your perfect itinerary and start exploring**. I promise, once you visit Durham, you'll be planning your next trip before you even leave!

Conclusion

As I sit here, reflecting on everything I've shared about Durham, I can't help but smile. This city has a way of **staying with you**, long after you've wandered its cobbled streets, listened to the cathedral bells, or watched the sunset over the River Wear. It's the kind of place that **invites you in and makes you feel at home**, whether you're here for a day, a week, or a lifetime.

I hope, by now, you're feeling **excited, inspired, and ready to experience Durham for yourself**. Because, no matter what kind of traveler you are—history lover, foodie, adventurer, or simply someone looking for a peaceful escape—Durham has **something truly special waiting for you**.

A City That Feels Like a Story

One of my favorite things about Durham is that it feels like **a living, breathing story**. The kind where **every street, every hidden alley, and every riverside path has something to say**. Maybe it's the **whispers of the past**, carried on the wind from the towering cathedral, or the **laughter of students**, filling the air in cozy cafés. Maybe it's **the warmth of the people**, who are always happy to share a tale, a tip, or a friendly chat over a pint in a centuries-old pub.

When you're here, **you become part of that story**. You don't just visit Durham—you **experience it, feel it, and carry it with you**. And that's what makes this place so unforgettable.

Why Durham Should Be Your Next Adventure

I could list a hundred reasons why you should pack your bags and come to Durham. The breathtaking **views from the castle**, the **hidden cafés**, the **cultural festivals**, the **stunning countryside just a short drive away**. But the real reason? **Because you deserve to experience something magical.**

Life gets busy. We get caught up in routines, responsibilities, and to-do lists. But every now and then, we need a place that **reminds us to slow down, explore, and simply enjoy the moment**. Durham is that place.

Here, you can wander without a plan and still stumble onto something

wonderful. You can take an evening stroll by the river and feel like you've stepped into a painting. You can sit in a historic pub, surrounded by stories centuries in the making, and feel **connected to something bigger**.

What Awaits You in Durham

So, if you're wondering what's next, let me tell you: **Durham is waiting.**

It's waiting for you to **stand in awe beneath the cathedral's towering arches**. It's waiting for you to **sip coffee in a quiet bookshop**, to **laugh with the locals in a lively market**, to **discover a hidden corner of history that makes you pause and take it all in**.

And when you do, I promise—you'll **fall in love with it** just like I did.

Until We Meet Again...

As you close this guide, I hope you carry with you **a sense of excitement, possibility, and curiosity**. Durham is a place to be **discovered, cherished, and explored**. But most of all, it's a place to be **experienced, firsthand and with an open heart**.

So, whether you're already planning your trip or just tucking this guide away for a future adventure, know this: **Durham will be here, waiting to welcome you**.

And when you finally arrive, **I hope it feels like coming home.**

Printed in Dunstable, United Kingdom

67641918R00087